FAITH MAN

Wild Adventures with a Faithful God
– the Story of David Lamb

DAVID LAMB AND RALPH TURNER

malcolm down
PUBLISHING

Copyright © 2019 David Lamb and Ralph Turner

23 22 21 20 19   7 6 5 4 3 2 1

First published 2019 by Malcolm Down Publishing Ltd.
www.malcolmdown.co.uk

The right of David Lamb and Ralph Turner to be identified as the
authors of this work has been asserted by them in accordance with the
Copyright, Designs and Patents Act 1988.

All rights reserved. No part of this publication may be reproduced,
stored in a retrieval system, or transmitted in any other form or by any
means, electronic, mechanical, photocopying, recording or otherwise,
without the prior permission of the publisher.

British Library Cataloguing in Publication Data
A catalogue record for this book is available from the British Library.

ISBN 978-1-912863-08-2

Unless otherwise indicated, Scripture quotations taken from

The Holy Bible, English Standard Version. ESV® Permanent Text
Edition® (2016). Copyright © 2001 by Crossway Bibles, a publishing
ministry of Good News Publishers.

Some names have been changed to protect their identities.

Cover design by Esther Kotecha
Art direction by Sarah Grace

Printed in the UK

Commendations

I'm not one for reading many books, so when I tell you that at least three cups of tea went cold because I couldn't put this book down you'll hopefully understand when I say it was gripping from start to finish.

I first encountered Dave's ministry as a young pastor at a leader's conference at Kingdom Faith in 1993. I remember being impacted by his relationship with the Father. I remember thinking, 'This man is a "friend of God" and I've just heard the real deal!' The Spirit's life, joy and fun just poured out of him as he ministered; clearly his Christianity was an ongoing adventure which was contagious. So, to read the 'before and after' of Dave Lamb's life for me was a delight.

One day without a miracle for Dave Lamb would be a boring day! And if anyone reading this has settled for a Christianity which is dialled down to what is just humanly possible, you will be challenged – in a good way! God really is the same yesterday, today and forever. He's the same 'God of Wonders' of Moses' time and he is the same God today as in the Acts of the Apostles… and Dave Lamb's life clearly demonstrates this fact.

Dave is one of God's men to raise up a new generation of evangelists that preach the gospel, not only with words but with signs and wonders following. Dave also talks candidly about the victories and the mistakes in ministry in a refreshing way that gives hope to us all. I love his honesty and humility as he spares no personal detail regarding the condition of his heart in times of

3

trial. Great anointing and a great ministry also come with great personal cost and suffering.

Dave and his wife, Joyce, have proved that absolute dependence on God for everything is the authentic lifestyle that releases the supernatural of heaven into our world. *Faith Man* is a must-read but beware, it will compel you to your knees to cry out to God for revival.

Mike Vickers, Senior Pastor of Stronghold Church, founder of Cross the Nations

David Lamb is widely known for his faith living. His writing captures the sheer essence of what it means to live by faith. It is a must-read for those who need encouragement, while going through adversity, knowing that the Lord will never leave us or forsake us. It gives us confidence in this day and age to know that we can still see miracles and breakthrough, just as in biblical times! So, if you want to see how faith as small as a mustard seed can move mountains, then this book is for you.

Revd Dr Jim Master, Senior Minister, City Life International Church, Sheffield

What a great story of God's transforming power. The Lord took David Lamb's problem-filled life and changed him into a man of faith and power. I had the pleasure of working closely with David for several years and I have always admired the anointing God has put on his life to preach, pastor, prophesy and move in the miraculous.

Anyone who reads this book will be encouraged and inspired

to move into greater exploits in God. I strongly recommend this book to all.

Ian Christensen, Senior Pastor, New Life Christian Centre International, Wembley

I have known David Lamb for many years. He is, as the title of this book suggests, a 'man of faith'... believing, active, miracle-working faith. Such faith is, of course, born out of a close personal relationship with God nurtured in the secret place of prayer. I highly commend David, and his book, to you... his life is a worthy example to follow, as you too embrace the adventure of 'living by faith'!

Jonathan Conrathe, Founder, Mission24

David shares his life's story in a very personal way, offering many insights into how God leads us, changes us, and makes us fruitful. The faithfulness of God is seen in the good and challenging times throughout David's life which have changed him from a self-centred hoodlum to a compassionate world-changer. It's an enjoyable read that will inspire you to keep pressing on with Jesus!

Dan Chesney, Senior Pastor, London Alive Church

David Lamb's story, *Faith Man*, is a riveting, modern-day book of Acts that will reignite your faith to believe that nothing is impossible with God! Pastor David's raw honesty as he shares his struggles and failures, as well as the dramatic miracles of his journey, impart wisdom and a deeper understanding of the Lord's great faithfulness towards those who are willing to surrender their lives completely to His purposes. Wherever you are in your own journey of faith, this wonderful book will encourage you to take hold of the promises of God, who 'is able to do exceedingly abundantly above all that we could ask or think'![1]

Karen Davis, Worship Director, Co-founder Carmel Congregation, Mt Carmel, Israel

This book is not just a story of David's life but it is a challenge for each of us to be a supernatural vessel of God! Many times, we think we need a God encounter that breaks us into this area of our life or we need a platform to facilitate it. In this book, you are going to find out how to have a supernatural lifestyle from a man that I have watched live this way. I believe that you will be encouraged as you read this book, but my prayer is that you will be mobilised after you read this book.

Dr. Sharon Stone, Senior Minister, Christian International Europe

---

1. Ephesians 3:20, KJV.

Thank you from David:

Joyce, thank you for our amazing journey together so far; without you none of this would be possible. What we have achieved has only happened because you're my wife and partner.

Thank you, Ralph, for extensive meetings with you and your delightful wife, Roh. Thank you for all the research and writing about God's miracles in my life.

Thank you to apostle Colin Urquhart for the thoughtful and inspiring Foreword. Thank you for those who took the time to read and commend the book; you are true friends whom I love. I can never forget Sarah who got on my case to write this book – thank you and well done for chasing a procrastinating lamb. Thank you, Jean and David, for the loan of monies to buy and sell this book, and thank you for those who pre-ordered.

Lastly, thank you to Father God and to my mentors: Revd Robin Rees, Revd Nicholas and Marigold Rivett-Carnac, Pastor Mike from YWAM, Pastor Ian Christensen, Philip Mohabir, Pastor Dan Chesney, Oliver and Margaret Nyumbu, Peter Carter, and the amazing prophetess Sharon Stone along with husband, Greg. Without wise counsel, tears, encouragements, rebukes and prayers, I would not have made it this far. You are all special to me and I love you all. (Nicholas and Philip are now with the Lord.)

Thank you from Ralph:

My thanks to Kim Connor and John Flavell who were my proof-readers. I so appreciated their thoroughness and excellent insights. Having John's involvement was quite poignant. His late father, Roger, was my friend and mentor for my first book back in 1993.

Grateful thanks to Malcolm, Sarah, Sheila and the team at Malcom Down Publishing. Thank you as always to my wife, Roh, for all her support, and her help with the interviews. And, of course, thanks to David and Joyce for letting me tell their story.

Books by David:

Keys to the Harvest
Angels & Demons

Books by Ralph:

Working for God
God-life
Cheating Death, Living Life: Linda's Story (with Linda Huskisson)
Gerald Coates: Pioneer
The Power Partnership (with Jonathan Conrathe)

Contents

Foreword

Dave Lamb is about to take you on a roller-coaster ride. This is an exciting adventure rather than simply being a book. You will be taken from one supernatural event after another, one miracle after another – all presented in a very readable form. So, this will encourage your faith!

The pace is breath-taking, but this makes the book more readable and the adventures more exciting. At the same time Dave is open and honest about the challenges and opposition he has had to face in the outworking of God's will for his life.

Joyce has been his companion throughout this roller-coaster ride with its highs and lows. There have been times of great anointing and blessing, times of needing to cry out to God in desperation. Yet through everything this is a wonderful testimony to the love, mercy and grace of the Lord Jesus Christ!

This is the kind of book that once you start the ride with Dave, you will want to continue to the end – not with regret that the ride is over, but with profound thankfulness to God for His faithfulness to His beloved children. We praise God for the innumerable people who have been blessed by God through the ministry of Dave and Joyce.

To Him belongs all the glory!

Colin Urquhart
November 2018

Chapter One
'The Devil's Got Me and He's After You'

I'm not sure how I made it up the street. I simply can't remember how I got home at all. I was high on amphetamines after an all-night drugs party. Approaching Mum and Dad's house, I wanted to be as quiet as possible. It was early morning and I was completely stoned.

I made it to the front door and even managed to work the door key. Then it was as quietly as possible up the stairs and into the bedroom I shared with my older brother Billy.

To my surprise, Billy was wide awake.

I loved my brother. He was fearless. He already had a reputation on our estate for being completely ruthless. A fighter. A part-time crook. And someone you didn't mess with. As hard as nails; even the police left him alone. I aspired to be like him.

But this morning, Billy looked different. There was fear in his eyes. It looked like he had been crying.

I rolled onto my bed and pulled up a blanket, still fully clothed.

'David. Dave! Listen! The devil's got me and he's after you!'

'What? What are you saying?'

'It's true! The devil's got me. And I can see what he's doing to you. Any more drugs and you'll be a goner, man! Look at yourself! You're as thin as a rake. You've lost your muscles. Your face is grey. Your skin looks pale. Davey, man, stop it before it's too late!'

I don't remember any more. I was too far gone to listen. I fell asleep and awoke to find I was on my own.

But there was a fear in the pit of my stomach. What if he was right? It was true, I was nineteen years old and I was out of control. Drugs had got hold of me. I was taking amphetamines most days – purple hearts and blues. More than that, when I got to the weekend, it was drugs parties at the squat. There were occasional outings on LSD – acid, as we called it. And if nothing else was available we'd get through a good amount of weed – marijuana.

As I lay on my bed that day, I knew I had to change. Change – or die. But what was I to do? I was a drug addict. Some of my friends were going onto harder drugs and it was hard to say no. What should I do? Where should I go to get help?

I remember praying. Not that I believed all that stuff. But I wanted help and was willing to try anything.

'God, if You're there, please help. I need help. I don't know what to do. Please, God.'

And with that I fell asleep again.

Bombed-out buildings

I remember my early childhood with affection. We weren't a bad family. Mum and Dad had come down from the north-east of England. Dad had been in the army before journeying south for work as a lathe-turner.

Dad could be stern on occasions and a bit undemonstrative. He wasn't particularly generous – or only when he was drunk – but he would always present his whole pay packet to Mum at the end of every week, giving all he could to the family. I remember him for his mild manners and non-confrontational approach to life. It meant I got away with a lot, though, and also meant that when I was looking to model my life on someone, I chose my much 'harder' brother Billy. I'd have been well-advised to have followed Dad's gentler example.

I wasn't that close to Dad, I guess. He could be a bit distant. A small, wiry man, he was a staunch trade unionist and although there had been a passing acquaintance with the Salvation Army, there appeared to be no real faith in God. But he did seem to respect my later Christian beliefs.

Mum was high-spirited, compassionate and loving. I was close to her. She worked as a maid in one of the big houses not far from where we lived. I never remember her as being tired, and despite the long hours, there was always a smile and a joke for me. She was always making ends meet. We weren't very well-off as a family. I remember many a meal based around soup from the butcher's bones, mixed with boiled barley.

I loved Mum and Dad. Even in my rebellious teenage years, I never really rebelled against them.

I was the youngest of five kids. Grace was the oldest. She was ten years older than me; sharp and sassy with a good sense of humour. Then there was Billy and after him, George. George wasn't like the rest of us. He seemed brighter; he tried harder at school. He didn't care for Billy's street gangs. Then, a couple of years older than me, there was Irene; sweet and vulnerable.

My earliest memories are down in Hammersmith. That's where I was born in 1945, part of the Baby Boom generation. I remember playing in among the bombed-out buildings after the war. I had a 'girlfriend' at the age of five and we decided to run away together. We made it to the next street before we were found and returned!

I was grounded, of course. But as soon as I was out and about again, I was back on the streets and then down to the local shop. A farthing would buy you two gobstoppers – one for each cheek.

If I wasn't on the streets, I would be upstairs, where my auntie Bella lived. We were close and I loved to visit, only avoiding her when her man was home – he was bad news, with a wild temper.

Fairhaven Crescent, South Oxhey is the real home I remember. That's where we were when I started school at Warren Dell, and then on to my secondary education at Clarendon School. And that was the same house I found myself creeping into that drug-induced morning.

Growing up with four older siblings had its disadvantages. I was always last to use the bathwater on our weekly bath night. I'm not sure I was any cleaner after the event than before! And I really could get dirty in the week, running wild in the streets and on the nearby golf course.

Some of us would play tricks on the golfers. With my friends Joss, Sal and Steve, I would wait for them to play their shots and then, while they were still out of sight, run onto the course and steal the golf balls. It was fun to hide in the bushes and watch as they forlornly looked everywhere.

Steve would often come back to our house and stay the night. Dad's comment, 'Two heads in the bed again, David,' was a pretty common one at the time!

Sunday school

Despite a distinct lack of belief, Mum and Dad used to pack me off to Sunday school once a week. I suspect it was simply a desire to get a bit of peace and quiet at home.

At a young age, I realised that when Dad had dropped me off at the front of the church building, all I had to do was pretend to go in, wait until he was out of sight and then go off and play. I was caught out the day I tried to climb a tree and ripped my best trousers. It's fair to say I felt the effects of my actions.

I don't recall any Sunday school teaching that really stuck with me on the occasions I did go into the building. However, rather bizarrely, my best subject at school was Religious Education.

Religious Education was the exception, though. I enjoyed English, but pretty much any other subject was to be avoided. I didn't work hard and I don't consider I was a particularly gifted child. I was pleased to get out of school for good at the age of fifteen, in 1960, with little in the way of a formal education and a growing desire to get a job in order to make some money to fuel my drinking and my soon-to-be-commenced drug habit.

Football

Don't put the book down at this point... I'm an avid Watford Football Club supporter! South Oxhey was not too far from the Watford ground and I remember going to matches as a kid, with my older brothers and my friends Joss and Steve. In fact, Dad was often at the matches, playing in the brass band, and if he was there, we got in free of charge. I still support Watford today and any of my Facebook friends will be able to confirm my constant affirmation of their moderate success.

I was also quite a good player myself. I was fast. And I wasn't afraid to go in hard. Having played football for my school, I went on to form a local team and played matches on a regular basis during my teenage years. I loved those weekends. I loved it, whatever the weather. The smell of the grass, the mud on the pitch – all part of my love affair with football. The whole day formed itself around the match. I'd prepare the team, get them warmed up, give the pep talk, organise the referee – the whole thing. Football kept me out of trouble; most of the time.

The job

'Davey! Dave! I need you!'

Billy was shouting up the stairs to me. Mum and Dad were away and Billy had been restless all morning.

'I'm doing a job with Roy and Jack. I need you as a lookout!'

I suddenly felt very important. At fifteen, to be asked by Billy to help him steal goods was something I had aspired to.

My sister Irene was in the kitchen. At just seventeen, her first child was due any day now. Jack was her man. She gave me a look as if to say, 'You dare!', but I was in. I didn't need to be asked twice.

Jack was part of our gang that day, as was Roy – a slightly older friend who knew how to break into buildings with the minimum of fuss.

We used a van and a car. I was lookout in the car, with Billy driving. After dark, we approached the large electrical store from the rear, broke open the back doors and filled both the van and car with as much as we could within the ten minutes we had allowed ourselves.

I was scared, nervously looking around me from my vantage point by the back doors of the store. My heart was pumping. I imagined every noise was the police. I kept twisting my head this way and that, unsure as to where I should look. No one was around, though. There were noises off to my left, but as I looked, all I could see was a rather worse-for-wear cat on its night-time patrol.

Back in the car and van, we were excited. We were shouting and screaming with joy at our success. But Billy was driving too fast. As we went over a bridge, we skidded and hit the embankment. I shouted. Billy looked at me, alarmed. He was holding onto the steering wheel, trying to keep the car under control, but by now we were half way down the bank.

The car hit the river with a tremendous splash. I screamed. Billy shouted to get out. Thankfully, the water wasn't that deep and we both made it to the bank.

The van had stopped ahead of us. We abandoned the car, which had been stolen anyway, and, soaked to the skin, ran to the van. Most of the stolen goods were in the van, so we figured we hadn't lost too much.

It was Sunday afternoon at about 4pm when the police called. We were supposed to have 'fenced' the goods straight away – passed them on to a buyer. But they were still in the house. Roy was seen as the gang leader and got three years in prison. Billy got eighteen months in Pentonville Prison. Jack and I were not suspected and both of us kept clear of the case.

It shook me up. But not enough to stay straight.

Chapter Two
Detention

My aspiration to be more like Billy took a turn for the worse when I was arrested for breaking into cigarette machines. Stealing had become a regular habit; shoplifting and breaking into vending machines – especially cigarette machines, as I could easily sell these on.

I'd been arrested a few times. Usually it was just a night in the cells, my money being stolen by the police and some kind of warning. But this time, the law had caught up with me and I ended up being sent to a government detention centre; similar to a borstal.

It was the early 1960s and the government of the time had started to introduce a 'short sharp shock' treatment. With that in mind, after a short time at the remand centre in Enfield, north London I arrived at the gates of HM Junior Detention Centre in Kidlington, Oxfordshire. I was a cocky, know-it-all youth who wanted to show the other lads how 'hard' I was.

No escape

We were given brown, scratchy shirts and shorts to wear, and put to work. That first day, the sun was shining. I was hot and already itching in the rough shirt. Breaking from sweeping the yard and wiping my brow, I looked up at the high walls and barbed wire on top of it. I realised there would be no escape. I would have to fulfil the three-month sentence and make the best of it.

The experience nearly broke me.

There was a constant threat of menace and the guards were comfortable in issuing their own harsh treatment with their fists. We were woken at 5am and underwent a physical education session before breakfast. Bunny hops were the worst. We had to crouch and jump forward on our haunches. The ache in our muscles by the end of it was excruciating. We were regularly marched around the exercise yard, forced to march in time. Once I managed to tread on the heel of the boy in front. The guard noticed, and switched us around, encouraging the boy to deliberately step on my heel. By the end of the session, there was a copious amount of blood in my shoe.

We were double-marched to all our jobs. Many were connected to digging foundations and gardening. Others related to polishing already clean corridors. The worst was cleaning the exercise yard markings with a toothbrush. The guards were aware it was a crazy job but that didn't stop the punishments, should there be any dirt left on the paint markings by the time we had finished. We were regularly knocked to the floor by the guards and we learned quickly to stay still once we had fallen, and make out we were hurt more than we were, in order to avoid further punishment.

One guard was particularly malicious and hit us on our backs and backsides as we entered the showers, calling us the 'red-hand gang', due to the marks he made.

I was caught talking to another boy one day – this was not allowed during working hours. I was being critical of one of the guards. It was he who heard me and he called me into his office. I was expecting the worst. Instead he smiled, and told me that if he was causing me to complain about his treatment, he was doing his job and I would be different because of it. In a strange way, it brought about a friendship between the two of us and I was always grateful when he was on duty as the physical abuse would be less than usual.

We went to bed early and for the first month or so, it was hard not to hear the stifled sobs of the boys around me during the night. I contributed to that sound.

But surprisingly, we seemed to recover from the shock and, of course, became much fitter as well. By the end of the three months, I was as fit as I had ever been. As I walked out of the detention centre, I felt I had beaten the system and left unbowed and ready to recommence my life of crime.

The blood covenant

I'm not sure we really knew what we were doing. I'd been out riding with my best friend Steve and his girlfriend Sal. She had a horse we used to ride bareback – not that I was any good. I think we'd been watching a film about gangsters who swore to protect each other and we decided to do the same.

The three of us cut our thumbs and swore we would be there for each other as we mingled the blood. Steve and I went further. Home-made tattoos were becoming popular at the time, as was the craze to tattoo the words 'hate' on the fingers of your left hand and 'love' on the fingers of your right hand. In addition, I did a simple picture of a stick man in the guise of *The Saint*, a TV programme at the time, starring Roger Moore. Under the picture, I tattooed Steve's name.

We were so stupid. The tattoos flared up, scabbed over, and eventually left us marked for life. I always wanted to do everything to excess. I was wild.

Looking back on it now, I can see it is only God that pulled me back from destroying my life.

I see the tattoos every day. Hard to miss as they are on my hands and wrist.

Over time I lost touch with Steve and Sal, although through the wonders of Facebook, I made contact with Sal again quite recently. She married Steve, but as an alcoholic, he was not a good husband and eventually died from drink.

Deeper

I drank a lot too, but would never consider myself to have been an alcoholic. But what did make me an addict were the drugs. When I was growing up, running the football team, playing pranks with Joss, Steve and Sal, I always vowed I would never touch drugs. But without any anchor in my life, without direction and with nothing to live for, the resolve didn't last. It started with marijuana, but by the age of nineteen, it had quickly moved on to harder drugs. Amphetamines were easiest to get hold of. I experimented with LSD and one time had to have a friend talk to me all through the night or else I feel I might not have made it.

It did not act as an alarm call, however, and I moved on to heroin and cocaine.

One night I stumbled through the door and made it to the foot of the stairs. I curled up on the floor, under our enormous grandfather clock. High on both heroin and cocaine, I was in a bad way. Every hour, the clock boomed out and every hour I thought I was being taken to hell. I was hallucinating, shaking uncontrollably, but unable to move.

Mum found me there in the morning, called the doctor and quietly helped me back into the real world. This was the lowest point for me; not only becoming aware that my drug habit was slowly killing me, but having to admit it to my family.

'That's better than what you've got'

Billy was back out of prison by this time and living at home. During his time in Pentonville, he had been put in solitary confinement for trying to escape. He was given a Bible to read in his cell. And he did.

In fact, he read it three times, cover to cover, before coming out of solitary.

As I shared a room with Billy, it was impossible not to notice his own struggles – but also his new-found desire to read the Bible. He kept telling me that I needed to change. He kept reminding me that the devil had got him and he was after me. It was wearing to listen to, but at the same time, something was going on inside me.

It was hard to keep away from the drugs squat. It was hard to stay clean. But one whole week I managed it. And it was during that week I had the most amazing dream.

In my dream, I was standing on a hill. The wind was blowing strongly, pushing my hair into my face. But this wasn't just any hillside. As I looked I saw a sea below me, and became aware of a crowd around me. I glanced down at my clothes – I seemed to be wearing traditional Palestinian dress. Suddenly I realised where I was. These were the hills in Galilee. The dream was so vivid; I could even smell the grass and feel the spray coming off the sea, carried in the wind.

Then I saw Him.

Jesus was speaking and there was complete silence. Everyone was hanging on every word. Suddenly, Jesus stopped, turned His head, and looked at me. His eyes were piercing. I could feel Him looking right inside me. But despite the feeling that He knew everything about me, I also felt an incredible love and acceptance. It was as if He loved me *despite* knowing all about me.

I woke from my dream at about six in the morning. At that same moment, Billy, across the room from me, also woke up. He looked at me, smiled and said, 'That's better than what you've got!' And turned over and went back to sleep.

I was dumbfounded. I'd not told Billy about the dream. I'd just woken up. And there he was, confirming what God had done.

A little shakily, I got to my feet, went over to my wardrobe and opened it. I reached up to the top shelf, feeling with my hand until I caught the hard edge of something. My Bible from my Sunday school days.

Back in bed, I blew the dust off, and opened the Bible. It fell open at my dream. There in front of me was the story of Jesus feeding the 5,000 in the hills by the Sea of Galilee. Now God had my attention!

You'd have thought that would be enough for anyone. But there was more to come. Just to be clear I wouldn't miss it, God then spoke to me in an audible voice.

'David, if you go on the way you are going, you will go insane. But there is another way, which will lead you home.'

That was it. Just those words. By now, tears were rolling down my face. I was checking Billy was back asleep as, even then, I was trying to protect my hard nineteen-year-old image and not be seen to cry.

As I got up that morning, and remembered the words I'd heard, I knew I had to find where Jesus lived. That's the way I thought about it. God had said He would lead me home. But where was home? Where did Jesus live? I went to a Catholic service. I went to an Anglican service. But in both instances, it didn't feel to me as if Jesus was living there. I needed to keep searching.

It was around that time that I accepted a £5 bet that changed my life.

Chapter Three
The £5 Bet

My search for truth coincided with one of the darkest times in my life.

Billy took his own life.

He had sectioned himself into a secure unit in a mental institute, and it was there, on an evening when he had had enough, that he hung himself.

During the months leading up to his death, he had been in and out of the mental facility. He had harmed himself on a number of occasions. But he had also done a wonderful thing. He wrote to the Home Office setting out every crime he could remember committing.

The Home Office actually wrote back to him, giving him a free pardon. He joked with me that he had a free pardon from God too.

I believe he did. I believe that he was the first in our family to find a faith in Jesus Christ, and despite the sadness of his death, there was a genuine faith.

As for me, I was in a state of shock. This was Billy; my hero. The brother I had been closest to. The one I wanted to model my life on. His fearless bravado was now exposed for what it was – a cover-up for all the insecurities and fears he had in his life. How was I to react? I became depressed. It was as if my life had imploded. All the structure and meaning was removed in that instant. I found it hard to eat; difficult to get out of bed in the morning. I would wake and look over at the empty bed, and all the memories would come flooding back.

My dream helped; but only a little. My awareness that Jesus was real helped me to think through what was happening to me, and slowly I began to recover. I can't say that I began to pray, or to pursue any kind of Christian faith, but awareness that there was more to life was a help.

I needed to move on. I had left school with just one O level in woodwork together with a modest record in crime. I was in and out of work and I needed a good job.

'You don't want to be doing this'

Billy was still alive when I landed my first job on a local building site as the 'junior', making teas and coffees. I wasn't very good at it and regularly got complaints from the workers.

But they also said something else which stuck with me. They could see what I, perhaps, could not. That there was more to me than a building site worker. They regularly used to encourage me to find a new and better job – not just because of my poor tea-making!

'Davey, you don't want to be doing this! You can do better than this.'

Eventually I decided to take them at their word and found a job spray-painting cars. That only lasted six weeks. A combination of arriving late for work and kicking a stone which smashed a car window saw the end to that career.

Through a friend, I was offered a job with a London-based window cleaning company. This was a big business, and for the next few years I worked as a window cleaner, both locally and in the centre of London. It brought in a steady income – not that I was keeping much of it. Some went to Mum and Dad, as I was still living at home, but most was lost on drink and, before I had my dream, the start of a drugs habit.

With Acme, I worked in some surprising places, none more so than St Bernard's psychiatric hospital. The patients on one occasion managed to get to an outside window on the highest floor and started to push the ladder away from the wall. Thankfully, they were not successful.

Despite a good seven to eight years working as a window cleaner, the words from the building site kept coming back to me: 'You don't want to be doing this.' There was something inside gnawing away at me. My hero and oldest brother was still in and out of prison, and beginning to demonstrate signs of the depression that would later cause him to take his own life. My other brother, George, had shown that it was possible to get on in life, and that was a challenge to me as well. My sisters were mothers early on in their adult lives and I was aware of their own frustrations with the choices they had made.

But what to do? How to be fulfilled? The drink and drugs weren't the answer. What was?

Getting darker

You know the saying, 'It's always darkest before the dawn'? That's true for me. Despite the job and the dream, I started to look in another direction entirely for my spiritual source.

One day I walked past a church and decided to go inside. Still looking for where Jesus lived, I thought this church might have the answers. The sign on the door said it was a spiritualist church. I had no real idea as to what that was, nor that it was a 'church' that was different to the normal sense of the word. I was welcomed and became a part of their congregation very quickly. They taught a lot on spiritual healing.

It was there I met Alice. Alice was a psychic healer and medium. She was especially good as an astrologer. Once she went into a trance and accurately told me all of my life up to that point. I was impressed.

'There's more I could teach you,' she said. 'Why not come with me to the Rosicrucian meeting?'

'What's one of those?' I said.

'Come along and find out!'

The secret order

The Rosicrucian meeting was fascinating and I was hooked. They taught through a series of weekly studies. This started off as something that seemed akin to humanitarianism, but it quickly took a darker turn.

Soon I was studying the occult, and metaphysics, and interacting with their twelve 'cosmic masters'. These were invisible 'masters' who guide the Rosicrucian Order. I became a vegetarian. I studied the darker arts and was soon proficient in palm-reading. I studied how to see through a 'third eye', a mystical, supposedly spiritual eye that is meant to lead to inner realms and spaces of higher consciousness. I travelled to Glastonbury to take part in the rituals, on one occasion witnessing the whole sky lit up with shooting stars as a goat was sacrificed.

A trip to Foyles bookshop in London furnished me with further reading material on the occult and on mystical meditation. I learned to meditate and 'channel' the 'life forces' into my own body, discovering how, as I thought, to master the elements around me, making for a better life.

But I still struggled. Something inside me told me that what I was now studying was wrong; that it did not lead to life and had nothing to do with the God who had spoken to me in my dream.

For three years, I participated in these dark rituals and practices, becoming part of a secret order. I was off drugs, but into something altogether more sinister.

'You're a loser'

My friend Phil and I nearly joined the army together. I was too young at the time, so was asked to come back in six months. I never did.

Phil came out after a few years with a serious injury and became a hospital ward orderly. We met regularly down the pub. I was clear of drugs. The dream about Jesus resulted in me never taking drugs again – never wanting to take drugs. It was as if the dream washed away all desire for drugs.

But without a Christian faith, the gap needed to be filled with something. If it wasn't to be drugs, it would be drinking with Phil. Serious drinking too.

On one particularly drunken night, Phil leaned over to me.

'David, I want to bet you something.'

'What's that?'

'It's this.'

He cleared his throat and looked me straight in the eyes.

'You're a loser, Davey. You're going to stay a window cleaner forever if you don't do something. I want to challenge you…' He leaned closer to me, almost falling off his chair. I could see the pock marks on his round red face as he came closer still. 'You're always going on about helping people. You're always complaining about life not being fair. So, do something about it!'

He had my attention and I was still sober enough to understand him. I had indeed complained on a number of occasions about the unfairness of life, how some people make it and others were trodden on. I wanted to do something about it, but with drink and drugs to the fore, I never had.

'So do something!' Phil said. 'See that hospital down the road? The one I work part-time at?'

'Yeah.'

'They were advertising for ward orderlies for their geriatric ward. Get down there and sign up! Problem is, you're all talk. I challenge you!'

By now Phil's voice had got quite a bit louder and others were beginning to listen in.

'I challenge you… go down there and get the job. I bet you £5 you never will!'

'OK, Phil. I will!' I said it with all seriousness. Through my drunken haze, I was ashamed by what he had said. It was too close to the truth. I *was* a loser. I *was* all talk.

And I was serious. Embarrassed, too. In my drunken state and with others listening in, I didn't want to look foolish. Plus, I really had talked of helping people. But most of all, it was the bet. I couldn't resist a bet and always wanted to take on a challenge. Even when it was only for £5.

That £5 bet changed my life.

The same week, I resigned from the window cleaning company and walked down the road to Abbots Langley Hospital. One interview later and I was starting work as an orderly – on the grottiest of wards. The patients I was looking after were for the most part beyond caring. It was very much a 'muck and bullets' job as I called it. A lot of bedpans. A lot of cleaning up messes.

I hated it.

But a bet is a bet. I had to win it, and Phil had put a time limit on it of a number of months.

The offer

Then something remarkable happened. I was transferred to another ward. This one was in the modern wing of the hospital and the patients were much more interactive and better behaved. And I loved it!

I loved it so much that I came to the attention of the senior sister on the ward. One day she took me aside.

'David, I want to talk to you about something. You're good at your job. You obviously love the patients, and they love you too. Why not train to be a state enrolled nurse? You could do it; I'm sure you could.'

I sat there transfixed. Was it just six weeks ago that I had responded to Phil's bet? And here I was being offered training to become a nurse. Me. Dave, the window cleaner. It seemed remarkable. It *was* remarkable!

'But I haven't done any studying in years. I have no exam passes...'

'Well, give it a go. Try the initial test and if you pass that, we'll take you on.'

'Why are you showing such interest in me?' I looked at her suspiciously.

She smiled.

'Actually, my husband knows you. He's a policeman, and the last one to take you to court for drugs possession.'

I'm not often lost for words, but that was one of those moments. She went on.

'I'm impressed with you. I've seen you change, even in the short time you've been here. My husband and I want to help you – help you to make something of your life.'

I felt close to tears. I couldn't cry, of course; not the hardened criminal I thought myself to be. But something was getting through. I remembered the prayers to God in the dark moments. I remembered the thoughts that there should be more to life. I remembered the dream. And most of all, I was overwhelmed that a couple who didn't know me cared enough to help.

I coughed, made my excuses and left. But that was the start of a new life for me. It came in stages. It certainly wasn't as dramatic as a single moment in time. But I took the test, passed it, enrolled as a trainee nurse – and began to change.

All because of a £5 bet.

Time to change

As I began the training, I spent quite a long time looking back on the previous couple of years. It was not good viewing.

A year or so before my conversation with Phil, I'd nearly lost my life. I was high on drugs, in possession of drugs, and running away from a couple of policemen who were chasing me on foot. I leapt a fence next to the railway line and quickly buried the drugs. They were mainly prescription drugs I used to pick up cheaply from a corrupt doctor in the East End of London.

What I hadn't noticed as I leapt the fence was the razor wire on the top. It cut deeply into an artery and by the time the police arrived, I had lost a lot of blood, with a stream of it pouring out of my arm like a fountain. Not that I had felt a thing. Being high means you are often not aware of any pain.

The policemen assessed the situation, told me they were abandoning the drugs chase but that they needed to get me to hospital straight away. Despite the blood loss, I remained conscious and got to the hospital in time. It was a close thing. I had nearly lost my life, and as I reflected on it at the beginning of my nursing career, I felt almost like praying a prayer of thanks to whatever God was there and helping me.

I still remember the incident every day. As I look down at my arm, you can still see the scar from the fifteen stitches.

Drugs and drink had taken over at that time. What had started as a weekend habit had progressed to taking over most of the week. I can't really recall how I did my job as a window cleaner, how I didn't fall, how I even made it to work in the first place.

The dream effect

My dream changed that. It was so startling. Even though I was not really aware of its full significance, it did something in me. It stopped my craving for drugs dead in its tracks. I can truly say that since the dream, since looking into the eyes of Jesus on that Galilean hill, I have only ever taken drugs the once. It was soon after and it was so ineffectual, I never bothered again. Looking back, God was at work in me even before I had made any significant commitment to Him. Now, with my enrolment as a trainee nurse, I found that not only was I able to stay away from drugs, but my whole body was beginning to change. I was gaining strength and weight – both of which I sorely lacked in my drug-taking days.

The dream was still bugging me in another way. Maybe there was something in this Jesus stuff? But what? And how to find the answer?

As I started training as a nurse, I began to realise that I wasn't going to find the answers in the occult and the Rosicrucian movement. I dropped off attendance – partly because of a growing awareness I shouldn't be going down that route; partly due to the hours of work that meant I had time for little else in the early days of training.

I did find time to go over to one of the squats on a Saturday night. Joss and another friend, Ian, were there. Both were mainlining heroin by now, having moved on from softer drugs. Being 'clean' meant that I noticed things I hadn't seen before. First of all, the squalor of the squat itself. Everything was filthy. How had I not noticed? And then the smell. There was an overpowering smell of stale food and urine.

Joss and Ian were both out of it. And offering me a fix. I had the willpower to decline, spoke for a moment about giving up and encouraged them to do so. But without conviction. If it were not for the dream, I would not have had the willpower to say no myself; how could I start telling Joss and Ian to stop?

I found myself praying again. Praying to the God who had told me to find where Jesus lived. Praying to the God who gave me the dream.

'Please, Lord. Help me. I've escaped drugs and the occult. But I'm afraid to get out of control again. I don't know what to do. I don't know where I'm going. Help me, God. Help me.'

Chapter Four
'You're Not One of Them, Are You?'

It was two weeks into my nurse training when I walked through the hospital cafeteria and saw them – two beautiful Malaysian trainee nurses sitting together on the right-hand side of the room. There were a few other tables available, but I acted as if I couldn't find anywhere to sit, and joined them.

Joyce and Fatima had just arrived from Malaysia and were, it turns out, on the same course as me. We chatted for a while and I asked them what had taken them from their homeland to the UK. I wasn't expecting the answer Joyce gave.

'I'm a missionary. I'm here to tell people about Jesus.'

I had two immediate thoughts. The first was along the lines of: 'Do we need missionaries in the UK? Aren't we supposed to be a Christian country anyway?'

The second thought was a little more basic: 'How come she is so beautiful?' My picture of Christian women at that time was of someone rather formally dressed with a high neckline and a tight hair bun. Suffice to say, Joyce didn't look at all like that!

'You're not one of *them*, are you?' I said.

'One of what?'

I didn't hold back.

'Christians. Fuddy-duddies. Stuffy know-it-alls.'

Joyce just smiled. 'Yes, I am. A Christian, that is. I'm not sure about the rest!'

'Why do you want to waste your life on that stuff? The Bible is full of fairy tales. There's better things you can do than that.'

Looking back, I was being aggressive because I was automatically in a defensive mode.

It was several years on from the dream and even though by now I was less engaged with them, I had thought I'd found my 'god' in the mysticism and occultism of the Rosicrucians. I didn't want to be told I was wrong.

Conversations went on over the next few days. Joyce introduced me to Devi, another Christian from Malaysia. I was quite attracted to Devi, so I began to pay more attention to Devi and Joyce and what they had to say as a result.

The Living Bible

Some time later Joyce's mum came over to visit and presented me with a gift – The Living Bible. It was a new Bible translation. I was a bit shocked to receive it and wasn't sure I should. But just to be gracious, I took it. I figured I could always ditch it later.

But I never did throw it away. That night, back in my nurses' accommodation, I began to read. This was different to the formal, old-fashioned language of my Sunday school Bible. It was easy to read. In fact, it was riveting.

I had read right through Matthew and Mark before I slept that night. The next morning, I started on some of Paul's letters. Wow! He had done some amazing things, and wrote in an incredible way.

One evening Joyce and Devi came to visit. They noticed the Bible on my bedside cabinet.

'So, you're reading the Bible then!' said Joyce. I could have sworn I heard an element of triumph in her voice.

'Not really,' I said, as casually as I could.

But the truth was, with four women praying for me – Joyce, Devi, Debra (Joyce's sister, also a nurse) and Joyce's mum – I really didn't stand a chance. Looking back on it now, I wasn't aware of their prayers at the time, but there is no doubt I had an increased sense of God speaking to me.

'I want to go to church'

Joyce was being very clever in the way she was encouraging me to consider the Christian faith. She would usually let me lead in conversations and then she would subtly steer us onto the subject of Jesus. One day she left a magazine on my table.

'What's that?' I said.

'Oh, nothing. You won't be interested,' said Joyce.

Of course, she knew that this would pique my interest, and sure enough, as soon as Joyce had gone that evening, I picked up the Christian magazine and began to read. There was an article on the Second Coming of Christ that particularly fascinated me. I had been thinking a lot about the end of the world, having heard a lot of strange teaching from the Rosicrucians. As I read, it all began to make sense. Of course, if Jesus was real, the only way to sort out the mess and constant war and destruction would be a new heaven and a new earth.

The next night, I announced to Joyce that I wanted to go to church.

'I'm on shift on Sunday,' said Joyce, 'so I can't take you. But how about you go with Joyce G, the sister on the main wards?'

That Sunday, Joyce G arrived in her Morris Minor, and drove me to her house, where I met a number of other people. They all seemed very pleasant, but I was feeling uncomfortable and regretting my decision to attend.

Then it was over to the church building – the Elim Church in Watford. To my complete horror, Joyce G took me right to the front and sat me on the first row. There was to be no escape.

I enjoyed the singing. I guess I'd call it worship today, but for someone without a faith, I was simply observing it. I don't remember the words of the songs particularly, but I do remember looking around at the congregation and wondering what they were on! There was such enthusiasm, such passion in the singing. I genuinely thought some of them must be on drugs.

Following the singing, the preacher got up to speak. His name was Robin Rees. Originally from Wales, he had moved to Watford to take on this particular church.

'I want to talk tonight about the Second Coming of Jesus Christ.'

Really? I couldn't believe what he had just said. The very thing I had been reading. The very thing I had been grappling with. And here was the preacher talking about it. I couldn't help thinking it was some kind of set-up! But how? Surely Joyce and Joyce G hadn't planned it somehow? Did Joyce know that I would be fascinated with that particular article in the magazine? Surely not? I hadn't even mentioned it to her.

Of course, it was God's set-up. At the end of the preaching,

I was caught. I had heard enough. As soon as the invitation to become a Christian was made, my hand went into the air.

Actually, my hand went down pretty quickly too, as I began to think through what I was doing. What would my friends think? Was I going just a little bit mad in responding?

But as I took my hand down, I found it going up again. God was on my case. I had found where Jesus lived and I needed to respond.

A few minutes later, I was in the small room at the back, with Robin, and on my knees. That night in March 1973, two months from my twenty-eighth birthday, was my turning point. All I had ever done, thought and planned was leading up to this moment. I knew I had found the truth.

'David, I want you to pray after me: Lord Jesus, I'm sorry for living my own way. Please forgive me. I ask You to come into my life, to live in me and to change me. Thank You for Your new life. Amen.'

And that was it. I didn't feel any great emotion. The clouds didn't open. Jesus didn't show Himself. I didn't get any new dreams that night. But I knew. I knew for sure that God had just changed my life. I had changed. The old David had gone. The drugs, the drink, the lying, the occult involvement. Everything had gone. I was twenty-seven years old and I'd just been born again.

A changed world view

As I woke the next morning in my nurses' accommodation, I knew I had changed. The first thing I noticed was that I was not swearing under my breath. My language had changed.

Then I began to think about what had happened the night before. I suddenly had such a compassion for my friends and family – anyone who didn't know what I had found. It burned within me. Others needed to know.

Other changes became clear over the next few days. I could no longer tell jokes at the expense of the Irish, Blacks or Jews. My world view had changed. My thinking towards everyone had changed. I wanted to read the Bible. I wanted to go to church. I wanted to be with Christians.

I began to deal with the anger and lust that had such a control of me. I began to get prayer for the effects of the occult. It took time. It took prayer and deliverance ministry – specific prayer and Christian ministry dealing with the things that had until that time had a hold of my life. Many of the older folks in the church decided to pray for me. They could see I needed radical change in my life. Their prayers worked.

A lot of my early encouragement came from Joyce G and her friend Anthea. Joyce, Devi and I would go over to their 'House of Healing'. Most Sundays we would be over there, outside of the church meetings themselves. There were about fifteen of us on an average Sunday at the house. I learned to wash dishes! Coming from a home where men stayed away from the cooking, I had managed to avoid the kitchen up to that point in my life. I had seen it as a place for women. All this changed.

More importantly, Joyce G and Anthea invited us to pray together and to study the Bible. As I studied, the Bible became more and more of a living document. No longer just words, but words with meaning, with application, and an encouragement to change my life.

Telling others

I had to tell others about my new-found faith. I couldn't do anything else. It was as if that was all I could do and all I wanted to do. With my every waking moment I had such a desire to talk about Jesus. When on the wards at the hospital, I developed a system to ensure that as far as possible every single patient heard about Jesus. Often it would be at bath time. Away from the ward itself, I would tell the patient what God had done for me – how I had been delivered from drugs, how God had set me free. Many came to Christ while I was washing them.

One evening Joyce G was the sister on the ward. She was asking one gentleman whether he would like to take communion the next day, when the local vicar would be there.

'Sister, I have just had a service in the bathroom. That will be quite enough for me at the present, thank you.'

Joyce G pursed her lips and looked over at me with a raised eyebrow.

Mini-revival

Something happened over the next few weeks that I can only record here as a 'mini-revival'. Nothing short of that can describe it. It was a sovereign move of God among the patients and the staff at the hospital where Joyce, Joyce G and I worked – and a similar move of God at Watford Memorial Hospital, where Anthea was a sister. Anthea saw around fifty (mainly staff) find a faith in Christ. I can't remember how many we had at Abbots Langley Hospital, but it must have been more than 100.

We were regularly taking staff and patients to the meetings at the Elim Church. Robin Rees was seeing many of them change their lives. We took Hindus, Buddhists and Sikhs to our meetings and most of them found a faith in Christ.

One young man from a Buddhist background was rolling around the floor in one of the meetings in seeming agony, until God touched him and released him from whatever tormenting spirits had been affecting his life. He lay still on the floor for a long time. When it came time to go home, we had to carry him out to the car. His body was as stiff as a board, as God continued to work, through the power of the Holy Spirit.

We showed the *Jesus* film one night. The film reached the point where Jesus was being scourged, before going to the cross. A young Hindu man that we had brought along stood up at that moment and started shouting at the screen, 'Stop it! Stop hurting Him!' Needless to say, the young man found a new life in Christ that same night.

I called at a friend's house. He was someone that had regularly been attending church but he had backslidden – gone away from his faith. I found him in bed, in agony with a painful back condition. I had called in order to 'tell him off' and try to make him see sense. But as I looked at him, I burst into tears. I had such compassion for him. I prayed a prayer of healing, along the lines of those taught to me by Joyce G and Anthea, and immediately he was healed. He was also healed from his backsliding and we saw him at pretty much every meeting after that.

The church was full. The House of Healing was full. Those of us in the nurses' accommodation found ourselves praying through the night for more to come to Christ. And as often as we prayed, God would answer and more patients and nurses found their way to the meetings and on into a new faith in Christ.

I was praying about anything and everything. Nothing was so small that God wasn't interested. Nothing was so big that God couldn't work. One time, I was due to meet my driving instructor in a large car park. The problem was that there were hundreds of cars. How was I to find him? I prayed, and felt God lead me through the cars. Sure enough, there he was.

The body cure

Then Joyce became ill. We prayed for her at the House of Healing, but nothing seemed to be working. She was diagnosed with a stomach ulcer – probably to do with the different foods she had been eating since arriving in the UK. A barium meal had been arranged to identify the extent of the problem. There was a significant ulcer, and as a result a new and strict diet.

It was during this time that we were all learning more about how God can heal people and with that in mind, Joyce sought out some prayer from the pastor.

The next day we were in the cafeteria and Joyce ordered fish and chips. One of the nurses from the X-ray team happened to be there and immediately pointed out to Joyce that she couldn't eat the meal because of what the barium meal had shown.

'But I'm healed!' exclaimed Joyce.

'Well, don't sign in sick tomorrow, then,' was the reply.

A week later, a second barium meal was arranged along with an X-ray.

'That's strange,' said the specialist. 'There's nothing there.'

The same nurse was there that had accosted Joyce in the cafeteria.

'She's from Malaysia. Maybe it's the Eastern medicines that have cured her?' said the nurse. 'And she's had the tablets from us as well.'

'But I haven't taken the tablets. And I haven't had any other medicines,' said Joyce.

The nurse counted out the tablets and they were all still there.

'What's really strange,' said the specialist, 'is that there is no scarring. If this ulcer has gone, there should be scarring. But I can't find anything at all.'

Joyce had received her healing alright. And all of us were encouraged to pray all the more for healing and salvation, as God continued to move by His Holy Spirit in mini-revival.

Joyce wore quite thick glasses. One day I told her to take them off and that I was going to pray for her eyes and she would be healed. Joyce duly did as I asked. I prayed, and she went off to work without her glasses.

'Nurse, where are your glasses? Why are you squinting?' said the matron.

'God has healed my eyes,' Joyce announced.

'Nonsense. Go and get your glasses!'

Joyce did so. But the strange thing was that when she put them on, she couldn't see!

A few eye tests later revealed that Joyce's eyes had been partially healed. She no longer needed thick lenses and much thinner ones were prescribed.

As I look back at our raw faith in those days, I can see we made a lot of mistakes. But mixed in with it was a simple faith, a mighty moving of the Holy Spirit, incredible healing and many coming to a faith in Christ. We were reading the Bible and believing the Bible. The Holy Spirit was doing the rest.

The praise cure

I found that being a Christian could be hard work. Keeping clear of temptation. Staying positive. Learning how to grow as a Christian. I owe a lot to Joyce G and Anthea at the House of Healing. Many times they would pray and minister to me. I received some more ministry, helping me overcome the bodily effects of the drug habits and the influence from the Rosicrucians.

Pastor Robin gave me a lift back to my accommodation one night.

'Pastor, I'm feeling really low. Almost depressed. What can I do about it?'

'Well, David, written on the soles of your feet, there are two words. One says "glory". The other says "hallelujah". What you do is put one foot in front of the other – and as you go, declare the words.'

So that's what I did that night. As I strode into my lodgings, I was calling out in step, the words 'glory' and 'hallelujah'. By the time I got to my room, I felt full of the Holy Spirit, on fire for God and ready to go on to all that God had for me.

And it turns out He had a lot for me to do.

Chapter Five
Feet Off the Ground

I'd been reading about the baptism in the Holy Spirit. Someone had given me a copy of *Nine O'Clock in the Morning*[2] by Dennis Bennett. It was a glorious read about how God moved in an amazing way in the life of Dennis Bennett, an Episcopal priest in California, and how whole communities were changed as people he helped began to understand that they could be filled with the Holy Spirit in a special way; how they learned that the gifts of the Holy Spirit listed in Paul's first letter to the Corinthians[3] in the Bible were still relevant today and how they began to speak in tongues and have their own prayer language.

As I read, I began to ask God for that same blessing. I'd wake in the morning and see if somehow God had moved on me in the night and I'd check whether I could now speak in tongues. When I found I couldn't, I'd ask God to do it there and then. I'd tense up and wait in anticipation – but nothing happened.

What I hadn't understood was that I needed to open my mouth to start speaking in tongues! Somehow, I thought it would happen automatically.

That Friday, I was able to get to the prayer meeting at church, and to my delight found that the pastor was speaking on the baptism in the Holy Spirit. Robin explained that we needed to take a step of faith and begin to speak out with a new language

2. Published by Kingsway, 1974.
3. See 1 Corinthians 12-14.

and that as we did, God would give us more and more words to speak. I didn't need a second invitation and that night I was gloriously baptised in the Spirit.

For me, it was the start of a six-month period in my life where I felt on fire for God. I was speaking about my faith at every opportunity and seeing many people find faith in Christ. My feet were off the ground. God worked through my life in so many ways. I expected every situation I faced to produce an opportunity to share my faith, and many times that was the case. In fact, it was such a disappointment when it didn't happen! I felt so close to God. I couldn't read enough of the Bible. I prayed every moment I had.

'You don't need it'

I was challenged in my new-found power partnership in the Holy Spirit by Joyce. She'd been brought up in the Methodist Church and didn't believe in the baptism in the Spirit.

'You don't need that!' said Joyce. 'It's not something for today. The Bible has taken its place.'

But Joyce was only speaking out what she had been taught, not out of what she was feeling in her heart. She could see the change in me. She could see how by God's Spirit, I had pretty much overcome my addictions and was on fire for God.

So, it wasn't that long before Joyce also received a glorious baptism in the Holy Spirit. Along with Joyce G and Anthea, Joyce and I were praying for every opportunity to share the gospel. I felt I had found my calling in life. I felt that this was why I had been born. This was why I had gone through such a hard time – I had a story to tell and I was desperate to share that story at every opportunity.

'I want to walk'

Arthur was in and out of hospital a lot. I could see him slowly going downhill over the year or so I looked after him. In the end, he was a shadow of the man I had first met. All skin and bones. Hardly able to eat and drink, he developed the 'death rattle' I had become familiar with as a nurse. It looked like he didn't have long to live, but at that point he had refused all my invitations to ask Christ to change his life.

Arthur had been a boy in the George Müller homes. There he had learned about God's provision. Often there had been no food on the table, but the boys learned to pray, and God answered. One time Arthur recalled a picnic hamper in the snow outside the front door, but there were no footprints.

Despite this, Arthur had lost his faith, and here he was near the end of his life and without faith. I felt led to pray and fast for Arthur. One night, I prayed for about half the night, on my knees, crying out for his salvation. The ward sister had called the family to come in and say their goodbyes the day before. He didn't seem to have long left.

As I finished praying in the middle of the night, I felt God say that the job was done. I slept a while and went back onto the ward as my shift started. As I gave Arthur a bed bath that morning, he looked up at me and whispered, 'I want to accept Jesus.' Tears formed in his eyes.

'Dave, I used to drink a lot. I wasn't good for my family; for my kids. Will He accept me?'

'Yes, Arthur, He will.'

We prayed together. Arthur asked God to forgive him and to

57

come into his life. That morning, I saw the change. He was more peaceful. He was ready to die.

But Arthur took me by surprise later that day.

'Dave, I've got a prayer request.'

'What's that, Arthur?'

'Will you pray for me, for God to heal me? I want to walk… I want to walk again.'

I had been certain he was going to die. His family had been in to say farewell. He'd had that death rattle in his lungs. But, I reasoned, God was more than able to heal, so why not? We prayed for a short while and I asked God for a supernatural healing. Nothing happened that I could see, and as I left the ward that night, I wasn't sure I would find Arthur alive the next day.

But he was. And he was sitting up in bed and eating.

Over the next two months in hospital, Arthur improved to the point where he was allowed to move to a care home. He came with us to church too, and would often be in tears, praying for the carers at the home.

'Dave, they don't believe me,' he'd say. 'They don't believe what God did for me.'

Arthur was a living testimony. The doctors couldn't explain it. One of them called him a walking miracle.

Dealing with the junk

Arthur was my first miracle. I began to get bolder with my prayers. My faith grew. But I was still struggling with the consequences of my choices earlier in my life.

'David, you need more help than we can give. We want you to

go and see some friends of ours.'

I was sitting in the lounge over at Joyce G and Anthea's house. They had been helping me through to a post-addiction and post-occult lifestyle. Many times they had let me stay over in the spare room, praying for me as I slept. Sometimes I couldn't sleep at all, in tears with temptations that felt so strong. The dream I had years before had dealt with any desire for drugs, but alcohol was still a problem, my dabbling with the occult caused me great stress, and I struggled with lust too.

I was aware of such a conflict inside me. On the one hand, I was desperate to spend as much time in prayer and Bible-reading as I could. On the other, my mind would be full of strange thoughts and ideas. I had just managed to avoid going to bed with one of the nurses who said she wanted to sleep with me. I had no idea how I had resisted, but I felt drained; almost shaken by it. Even more of a problem were the mind games I found happening as I tried to sleep. I would be taken back in my mind to séances I had been in and to fortune-telling words spoken over me. This caused me to lie awake for hours. And when I did sleep, there would be dreams. Dreams of falling off a cliff and feeling that if I didn't wake myself up before I hit the bottom, I would be dead.

Joyce G and Anthea arranged for me to visit a former captain in the Royal Navy. Jimmy and Fynvola James lived in Northwood, south-west of Watford. They were from an Anglican background and God had used them a lot in deliverance ministry. And it seemed I needed a good deal of deliverance.

God had got hold of me. The Holy Spirit was within me. And

in that respect, the devil had no control. But because of my past – the psychic readings and astrology, and especially my links with the Rosicrucian Order – there was no doubt that I was still struggling with some of those demonic effects on my life. It's not possession – it can't be if you are a Christian and have been baptised in the Spirit – but it is what New Testament Greek calls being 'demonised'. In other words, still affected by my past.

My time with Jimmy and Fynvola was so helpful. We prayed through a lot of things. I declared myself free from my past influences. Demons were commanded to go. And I came away free. I felt God had done a work in me, clearing out the junk.

Hours with God

I was free. But my faith in my own physical healing was all over the place. I had good days and bad days. Because of my drug abuse, I was still not in a good shape physically. Sometimes after work, it was all I could do to get back to my room and collapse on the bed. I didn't know what to do, except to pray. So that's what I did.

I prayed for many hours for my own healing, for the salvation of those around me. I'm not sure, looking back, how many hours I prayed each week, but it felt like pretty much all the time outside of my work and attending church. It was as if God was closeting me away.

And with that time with God came my own healing. I began to recover physically. My body got stronger. My desire for anything outside of God's will diminished. I got stronger in my mind. The truths of the Bible were beginning to get through. I sensed more and more that I had been saved for 'such a time as this'.[4] I was filled with the Holy Spirit, passionate about seeing people come to know Christ personally, and desperate in prayer for God to move.

I learned to read the Bible just before I slept, and in this way, I was preparing myself to hear God even when I was asleep. I dreamed one night of looking in at a beautiful garden. But the problem was that I was on the wrong side of the fence. As I looked, I saw a hole in the fence at the bottom. I crawled through and found myself dancing in this most beautiful of places. When I woke, I found that many of my cravings seemed to have left me in the night.

By God's grace, there was an overflow from those hours spent with Him. People began to ask why my prayers always seemed to get answered. Others felt God's presence when they were with me. Don't get me wrong; I was far from perfect. I still did so many things wrong! But I had been in His presence – and it changed me.

I was learning to listen to God in the daytime too. When I did something from my own good ideas, things didn't work. But when I listened and obeyed, God moved. God was speaking to me in so many different ways during this time. Directly through His Word. The whispers of the Holy Spirit when I prayed. Through being out in His creation. Even through comments from other people or by way of the things I read as I was out and about – advertisements and billboards became sources for God suggesting things to me.

---

4. Esther 4:14, NIV UK 2011.

And as a result, if I obeyed what I heard, I found God was ahead of me. Salvations followed. Healings followed. I was an apprentice in the best school in the world, listening to all God said.

Clearing my conscience

It was during this time that I attended a Selwyn Hughes conference. Selwyn was particularly good at explaining how we each needed to keep a clean conscience before God in order to know His closeness. I knew that's what I wanted. And I knew that's what I needed to do.

My first letter was to British Rail. I had smashed up some of their carriages in a drunken episode a few years earlier. I wrote to apologise and included a cheque to help pay for the damage. Their reply was similar in content to a number I received as I sought restitution:

Dear Mr Lamb,

Thank you for your letter. We are delighted that you are able to clear your conscience. Your misdemeanour was so long ago, we have no wish to press charges. However, we will accept your financial gift and put it towards one of our charities.

Thank you again for your honesty.

Yours sincerely …[5]

---

5. This is a paraphrase of the original.

Boots the chemist wrote a similar letter; I had written about all the low-level drugs I had stolen from them. I called in on my local Woolworths to apologise. The young store manager was rather nonplussed; not sure what to do. In the end, he accepted the money, and like other shops, put it into a charity the shop was supporting.

The owner of one local café was a little more upset, as he had trusted me. I had drilled into the side of a slot machine to rig the line-up of the pictures, and take the winnings. In the end, he also accepted my financial restitution.

The detective sergeant

It was a cold Monday afternoon when I arrived at the police station near to my parents' house. There was a strong wind, with showers of rain. The weather reflected my mood. I wasn't sure how this was going to go.

A detective sergeant agreed to see me and I began my verbal download of all the things I had done in the local area – the break-ins, the robberies, the fights, the vandalism. He listened open-mouthed as I related my crimes over a number of years.

'And why exactly are you telling me all this?'

'Because I'm a Christian now. I don't want these things left on my conscience. I want to be sure that as far as possible, I have paid for anything I did wrong.'

'Well, we're not going to charge you. It's all too long ago. But how about you and I take a drive around? You can show me the houses you robbed and maybe you can speak to the owners to apologise.'

And that's just what we did. Some were out. Many were at home and were happy to accept my apology. One lady, obviously a Christian too, grabbed hold of me and hugged me, whispering 'welcome home' as she did so.

It was a moving afternoon. None more so than for the detective sergeant. At the end of our visits, as we arrived back at the police station, he broke down in tears. He asked me to pray for him and especially to pray for his marriage. As I did so, I saw what appeared to be a cloud over him break, and his whole demeanour became lighter. Funnily enough, that afternoon brought about a friendship between the two of us that lasted a good number of years. If you would have told my teenage self that I would be friends with a policeman, I'd have told you where to go!

Martin

Martin was one of my drinking friends. We'd had a pretty nasty fight towards the end of my time in the squat. I'd hurt him a lot. When I went to see him to apologise, Martin's eyes grew wider and wider.

'Why are you doing this, man? What's got into you?'

I told him what had got into me – the love of Jesus Christ. As a result, he asked if he could come over to my church and sure enough, he did. I cried as he went to the front and gave his life to Christ.

I sought out other friends from my drugs and drinking days. Some responded, some didn't. But I continued to pray for them for many months following my visit; that God would break through in their lives in the same dramatic way He had broken into mine.

Life had changed. I knew my God. He was speaking so clearly to me. I wanted nothing more than to follow Him wholeheartedly. And with my conscience clear, and my past influences dealt with, it was as if God was saying, 'Now let's go on an adventure together, Dave…'

Chapter Six
Together

'Hey, Joyce. You know your friend Devi? I wonder whether we could go up to London to see her? I really fancy her. Do you think she'd go out with me?'

'I don't know... but you can ask!'

A few days later, Joyce and I were on the train. Devi was a lovely girl from Malaysia, of Indian heritage and a good friend to Joyce. I knew Joyce wouldn't mind me asking Devi out as Joyce herself had declared a few weeks earlier that she intended to be 'single for Christ'. In fact, Joyce had been engaged to a young man back in Malaysia – a kind of arranged marriage – but she had called it off following a chat with Robin, our pastor. It was clear that the boy in question was not a Christian and Joyce had decided to move forward with her faith and get baptised. This brought the whole question of her fiancé front and centre. Robin had gently suggested to Joyce that it may not be the best idea to marry someone without a Christian faith and expect that he would somehow 'convert'. Joyce had disagreed at first, to the point of cancelling her own baptism.

Baptism day

However, on the day of the baptism, God had spoken to her and she decided to go ahead, despite not having a towel or a change of clothes. What Joyce didn't know was that a friend of hers had been praying for her and had brought a towel and spare clothes in anticipation of God reversing Joyce's decision!

I was baptised on the same day. It was a glorious occasion. Much more than just a symbolic moment reflecting Christ's own 'baptism' into death, and His resurrection, but a time when the Holy Spirit moved strongly. As we came out of the water, we knew our sins really were washed away. We knew God loved us. And we felt the presence of the Holy Spirit upon us. Both Joyce and I knew we had moved forward significantly in all God had for us.

It was then, though, that Joyce declared that she was going to remain single for the Lord and would never marry. Hence, I had no problem in asking her if she could arrange for me to meet Devi.

I must admit that when I first asked, I sensed something of a hesitation in Joyce, but I put it to the back of my mind. She couldn't be upset that I liked Devi, could she? After all, she was destined to be single for the rest of her life. There was something, though; she just looked a bit uncomfortable about it.

On the train

I was nervous as Joyce and I arrived at Devi's. Joyce made an excuse to leave and I got some time with Devi on my own. I asked her if she would consider going out with me.

'David, you're like a brother to me!'

My heart sank. That was as clear a message as could be that Devi didn't have the slightest interest in me.

I was feeling pretty low on the train journey back.

'Never mind,' said Joyce. 'God has the right woman for you. We just need to pray.'

So, we did. There and then, on the train, Joyce and I prayed that God would find the right partner for me and that it would be so obvious I wouldn't miss it. I wasn't quite sure, though, why Joyce seemed unable to look me in the eye for the rest of the journey.

A few weeks later, and with Christmas approaching, a number of us in the church went out carol singing to some of the old people's homes in the area. After one of these evenings, I walked Joyce back to her accommodation and joined her in the common room for a drink before leaving. Joyce had a headache, so I took time out to pray for her.

That was when I knew.

As I finished praying, there was a silence. We looked at each other.

'Joyce, I know you said you were going to stay single, but… do you think God is doing something here? Something between us, I mean.'

Not the best chat-up line in the world. But the effect was clear.

There was a tear in Joyce's eye as she said, 'Yes.'

She'd known for a while, of course, but just hadn't said anything, asking God to make it clear to me. I had been a bit slow on the uptake!

We'd been best friends for a long time now. We had even been paired up in our nurses training. But I had never considered Joyce to be more than a good friend. The move from friendship to love had been gradual. I had to deal with my fear of commitment. Joyce had to deal with her concern that marrying a 'white man' always ended up in divorce – a view promoted every time she read the newspapers about yet another famous couple divorcing.

But that evening, just before Christmas 1975, we held hands. And we knew.

Growing together

Having been such good friends, our move from friendship to love was an easy one. We saw a lot of each other anyway, and often worked together. I used to go round to Joyce's flat whenever I could – not least because of the food she cooked! Although living in Malaysia, Joyce's family were from Sri Lanka. And most of the meals prepared in Joyce's kitchen were curries of different kinds. I loved it.

It wasn't all easy, though. As I mentioned, I had a fear of commitment. Three times I broke off our friendship, and three times God spoke to me that Joyce was the one. I remember Anthea helping and counselling me to keep going in my relationship with Joyce. I remember Joyce G wanting to hit me over the head with a rolling pin for hurting Joyce and breaking things off with her!

For Joyce, too, there were doubts. Prior to her sudden determination to be single, she had felt that God would give her a pastor as her husband – but I was a nurse. And if I had any call, I was looking to be an evangelist, not a pastor. Joyce felt God's assurance that I was the right man and that God would sort out the job description in due course.

Bible college

A friend had told me about a Bible college that I might be able to enrol at and still keep some employment. The thought had stayed with me ever since. Jean and Elmer Darnall, a dynamic American couple, had been making waves among the UK churches for some time, ever since their first visit in 1967. They now ran a Bible college which could be accessed by way of evening classes. I decided I needed to be there.

It took a big step of faith. In order to manage the flexibility and not be on shift work, I had to let go of my nursing career and return to window cleaning. I built up a new clientele and the money I received went towards the Bible college fees and living expenses.

I moved back home to cut costs down further and travelled up to the college near Kennington Oval in south-west London three times a week for evening lectures and exams.

When I wasn't studying or window cleaning, I was cutting my teeth as an evangelist. I'd been hesitant to accept the 'title' of evangelist as it seemed to me to be more appropriate to those I read of in the Bible. But that is what I was. I was consumed with telling others. There was nothing more I wanted. To be speaking of my faith was my 'sweet spot', the reason I lived.

I'd often be in the old people's homes, and occasionally on hospital wards when they would let me, speaking about Jesus. I began to preach in the shopping centres, standing on a corner, telling my story, inviting others to know Christ, offering healing and peace. It was a bit hit and miss. I was over-the-top on occasion, lacking any finesse in talking about my faith. But despite that, I was able to lead many to Christ.

I was heckled once by a man in one of the shopping centres. At that moment, God gave me a word of knowledge for him. A word of knowledge is described by the apostle Paul in his first letter to the Corinthian Church in the Bible.[6] It's something God drops into your mind about someone that you can't possibly know.

I went over to the man who had been shouting at me and spoke quietly to him.

'Excuse me, sir. God is telling me that you have just been left by your partner of many years. You're on your own and you're lonely and broken-hearted.'

He immediately broke down in tears and we were able to pray together.

My life developed a pattern. Study. Train journeys. Bible college. Window cleaning. Preaching. These were formative years with God helping me to learn how to walk with Him and how to talk for Him.

The angel

Joyce joined me at the Bible college after the first year and we studied together. We were now very much an 'item' and beginning to talk about marriage. We were planning to marry in Malaysia. And more than that, we were beginning to feel a call towards serving God in Malaysia in some capacity or other. It was all a bit vague to start with, but God began to put plans together for us – including a prophecy[7] from Jean Darnall.

The day for our commissioning at the end of the Bible college course was fast approaching, but as we got nearer to the day, I became very ill. Looking back, it seems to me to have been a final attempt by the devil and his minions to stop me from pursuing what God had for me.

6. See 1 Corinthians 12:8.
7. 1 Corinthians 14 speaks of the gift of prophecy.

Joyce gathered a few people to pray for me. While they were doing so, I was back home in bed. It was then – while they were praying – that I saw an angel. Not particularly big. Dressed in white with wings and standing at the foot of my bed. The angel was pointing, and in the Spirit, I somehow knew he was pointing to Malaysia. Then he blew a trumpet, pointed again, and said, 'Go!'

It was hard to miss the meaning! But I still felt too ill to go to the commissioning event. Joyce arrived and came up to my room. Without any hesitation, she came over to me, dragged me out of bed and told me God had healed me and I was to get dressed.

I didn't feel healed at all. In fact, as I got up, it was all I could do to stay on my feet. But then something remarkable began to happen. The more steps I took, the better I felt. By the time I had washed and dressed, I felt completely well.

That night, at the commissioning, Jean walked over to me and Joyce. She put her hand on my shoulder and started to speak.

'David, I know your links through Joyce to Malaysia, but I feel there is more than a link. I feel God is saying for you to "go". For the two of you to serve there. God is calling you to Malaysia.'

Chapter Seven
Malaysia

Both Joyce and I had been impacted by the stories of George Müller and his orphanages. In particular, we were impressed by the way he always prayed for money and food to come in, rather than ask for it. We needed about £1,000 to get us out to Malaysia to get married and agreed we would pray for the money to come in.

The next day a letter arrived from a friend with a cheque for £5 and an explanation that they had felt prompted by God to give. It was a small amount, but we were encouraged to know that God was on the case.

And He was! Money was given by friends at church. More arrived in the post. Then a friend felt to give £450. By then we had enough for the tickets and our adventure could begin.

The tickertape welcome

I had never flown before, so the flight itself was a real adventure. I was nervous, praying in tongues a lot at first, but gradually became used to the sensation of flying. As we landed, I became fearful again. This was a new country. In fact, every country was a new one, having never been out of the UK! I sensed, though, that God was in charge. And then an amazing thing happened.

As we walked down the steps of the aircraft, I saw something in the heavenlies. I saw myriads of angels around us, filling the skies. They were dropping tickertape down on us, with cheering and singing. Then I heard the voice of the Holy Spirit inside me. He said, 'Welcome to Malaysia, man of God.' It's fair to say that I felt anything but a man of God. At that point, I had hardly preached a sermon, I felt I didn't know the Bible at all well, and I was still feeling the nerves from the flight. But they were the words I heard. What a welcome! And what a confirmation to both my call to Malaysia in particular, and to the lifestyle of a travelling evangelist that I was about to step into.

Wedding day

We had flown into Kuala Lumpur, the capital of Malaysia, and were met at the airport by Joyce's family. There was an immediate shopping trip for a white sari for Joyce to wear at the wedding.

My senses were in overload. The colours. The noise. The traffic. I'd never seen anything like it. I loved it. There was something about the place that felt like home the moment I arrived. I remembered Jean Darnall's prophecy and wondered what God was about to do.

What God did first of all was to bless the wedding. Despite Joyce's father wanting her to marry a Sri Lankan, I was accepted into the family very quickly.

The wedding itself, in Joyce's home town of Ipoh, south-east of Kuala Lumpur, was a riot of noise and colour. Joyce looked amazing. And as part of the ceremony, people pinned money to her sari – so we then had enough to go off on a honeymoon.

The honeymoon was in Penang, a beautiful coastal area north-west of the capital. Pristine white sand beaches, beautiful food – and a beautiful bride.

The girls' school

Back from the honeymoon, Joyce and I immersed ourselves in the work we felt God had called us to. We went to an Assemblies of God church in the town, where Joyce's family had all found a faith in Christ.

I didn't know how to preach and had little idea how to prepare a sermon, but people were so gracious.

'David, just share your testimony. You have such a story to tell.'

So that's what I did. And God brought about amazing results.

Joyce came home one day with a triumphant look on her face.

'David, I've just got permission for you to speak at the school I grew up in. It's a girls' school. You're taking the assembly on Monday!'

This was it, then. One of the first times I was to speak publicly. And to such a large number.

I got up early that day. I could hear Joyce's mum already up and about in the kitchen below. I walked up the stairs onto the flat roof and began to pray. I was nervous. The sun was already up in a cloudless sky. I was distracted below by two mynah birds competing in a screeching competition in the garden trees.

'Lord, help me. I need to speak well today. I feel this is a first step for me with such a large number listening. Please give me the words to say.'

Dressed in a smart shirt and trousers, I walked with Joyce towards the school building. There was a big play area and next to it a beautifully managed lawn and flowerbeds. I could hear the chatter of the girls as I approached the red-roofed colonial building.

The cool of the building was welcome after the fierce sunlight. As I sat near the front of the assembly hall, I was introduced – and it was time.

I can't remember exactly what I said. But I do remember the results.

At the end of sharing my story, I asked if anyone wanted to become a Christian and if so, to put their hand up. Nearly every girl in the room responded. So many, in fact, that I wondered whether my invitation had been properly translated. But it had been and over about three weeks, we saw more than 400 girls find faith in Christ for the first time.

It was an amazing experience. It was a period of new birth. And it was a time of confirmation for me. This was what I was called to do. I could see how God was moving as I preached. I could see the results. I had no doubt that God was calling me to be an evangelist. If I had ever doubted it, the doubts were now well and truly gone.

The trick

It was a time of revival among the youth of the city. Hundreds were getting saved, with the meeting at the girls' school as a catalyst.

At one point, I began to get a bit big-headed. I was the person at the epicentre of the revival. I was being asked to preach in youth groups and churches. And then one day, God pulled me up short. It was on a return visit to the girls' school. I arrived early and walked into the room where the meeting would be. There at the front were five girls, all crying out to God. In tears, they were asking God to move. It wasn't only God that was moved – I was moved. I realised that this was the true centre of the revival. It was young people crying out to God that was causing the Holy Spirit to work so mightily. It was a timely reminder that it wasn't about me.

One day, I was approached by a Muslim teacher.

'David, I wonder… please could you tell me about your faith? And maybe, if you have a Bible to spare, please could I have one?'

Joyce was with me and was frowning. But I missed the signal. Malaysia is a Muslim country and it is illegal to convert a Muslim or to give a Bible.

I was excited. This was a Muslim man asking me about my faith. Then the strangest thing happened. As I tried to speak, nothing came out. I couldn't speak – and if you know me, you will know that was a miracle in itself!

I mumbled. I tried to speak, but nothing. The man frowned, looked at me strangely and walked away.

'David,' said Joyce, 'that was a trap! Don't you know he was trying to get you to give him a Bible? If you had, he would have reported you and we would have been expelled from the country.'

God had miraculously closed my mouth.

Still learning

I would do things differently nowadays, but in Malaysia, there was a sense that the devil was more open in the way he worked. There seemed to be a big need for deliverance ministry. Joyce and I had never operated in this ministry, and the only example I knew of was my own deliverance when I called on Jimmy and Fynvola James.

I commanded a demon to leave a lady and to my surprise, it seemed to go straight out of her – and into Joyce's dog! The dog started to run around in circles, growling. Then it got out of the house and started to attack another bigger dog in the street. I had to run out and separate them, and then commanded the demon to leave the dog. It did, and the dog, a little worse for wear, became docile again.

I know these things may seem far-fetched as you read them. It depends on what you've been taught and what you have experienced, but I have to say that throughout my ministry, I have witnessed demonic activity many times. But always, the name of Jesus is greater!

Chapter Eight
Transported

As Joyce and I walked out of Heathrow Airport, I was praying. We had been in Malaysia for two and a half months. Having done all we felt God was wanting us to do there, we were back. There was a problem, though – we had nowhere to live. Joyce's brother had flown back with us and had arranged to stay at a youth hostel, so I figured we should go there too.

The only problem was we couldn't get a taxi. There were enough of them around, but no one would take us.

'Sorry, mate. Too much luggage for me!' shouted one driver.

Another ignored us completely. Another drove towards us and then took off again. It was bizarre. Here we were at a taxi rank and we couldn't get a taxi!

It was then that I heard God telling me to call the principal of the Bible college we had been at. I was reluctant to do so. We had been following the George Müller principle and not making our needs known – and here I was being prompted by God to explain to the principal that we had nowhere to stay. I was faithful to the prompting and we walked away from the taxi rank to find a phone.

'David, that's amazing timing! We've had some students leave their accommodation just this morning. There's a flat free right next to where the Bible college meet.'

As we walked back to the taxi rank, I thanked God for His provision. The very first taxi to approach stopped for us and took us on our way.

The baronet

That first Sunday, we went to the Anglican church whose buildings hosted the Bible college. It was an amazing meeting. I had a picture in my mind as to what an Anglican meeting might be like, but this was not in line with that picture.

The vicar was Nicholas Rivett-Carnac and along with his wife, Marigold, they led a diverse and quite needy community at their church. Nicholas had worked at Holy Trinity Brompton church for a while, a hotspot for powerful Holy Spirit-led ministry, and they had brought that same ministry to St Mark's Church, Kennington. One of his first successes was getting most of his Parochial Church Council baptised in the Spirit. Nicholas was a baronet; a hereditary English title. But despite the title, he had felt God calling him to ministry and chose to follow God. With his exuberant nature and the open and unorthodox style of meetings, the local newspaper called him the 'dancing vicar'.

We were not aware of it at the time, but we were observing a church that had been used by God in a number of charismatic renewals. People were coming to the church from quite a distance. It had a reputation as a place of blessing. Many doctors and nurses visited from Guy's Hospital and other hospitals in the area. There was quite a mix of professionals as well as locals, plus many who were living rough on the streets.

As I looked around that morning, there seemed to be people from every possible background and many different nationalities. The service was vibrant and well-led. By the end of it, I felt I heard the Holy Spirit whispering to me, 'You're home now.' I didn't say anything to Joyce though.

As we walked back into the street after the service, Joyce turned to me.

'David, I think God was saying to me that we are home now. I think this is where we should be.'

I smiled.

The box at the back

It didn't take us long to get to know Nicholas and Marigold, and within a few weeks we were part of the leadership. I began to operate as their evangelist. We lived off whatever there was in the offering in the box at the back of the church building. Sometimes we lived well. Most of the time we survived.

During our time there, the church grew from a small congregation of fifty or so to more than 500, in addition to many more visitors. We worked through evangelistic home groups. Many found a faith in Christ – I estimate between ten and twenty people every month. We celebrated with meals at the church building, followed by a visit to the local Baptist church to get all the new converts baptised! During our time there, hundreds were baptised.

Miracles were breaking out in the services. We saw dramatic healings. Meetings would go on past midnight sometimes with many people getting baptised in the Holy Spirit. People fell under the power of the Spirit. There were prophecies, words of knowledge; it was a powerful anointing. And such a precious time for us.

I learned that it was less to do with the 'badge' on the building and much more to do with the leader and the team. Nicholas and Marigold had such a gentle ministry and a willingness to serve. In the most gentlemanly of ways, Nicholas ignored a lot of the Anglican protocols, so our meetings were informal and on fire. Worship was dynamic and word got around as to what was happening. Many people turned up for meetings, having heard of the move of God, and as a result, found healing and salvation.

Nicholas and Marigold became leading figures in the charismatic movement in the Anglican Church and were mightily used by God. I am so grateful that I heeded the prompting of the Spirit that time in the Heathrow taxi queue.

Bearing fruit

The apostle Paul says that the fruit of the Holy Spirit is 'love, joy, peace, patience, kindness, goodness, faithfulness, gentleness, [and] self-control'.[8] Unbeknown to me, God was doing a number on my life. By His Holy Spirit, He was changing me – including my attitude to Joyce. Being a mixed marriage at a time when there were few (and therefore few examples to follow) was hard. We were from such different cultures. And there is no doubt that I was overzealous in my new-found faith. All was for the Lord, of course. There is nothing wrong with that as long as we have enough maturity regarding how to apply it.

Banning Christmas because of its pagan roots was not my cleverest decision. When I realised what it was doing to Joyce, I repented of my wrong attitude and we began to embrace Christmas. I am so pleased I changed. Joyce's ability to decorate

8. Galatians 5:22-23.

the tree, to cook, to invite friends and to celebrate Christ's birth in creative ways has been such a blessing.

Anger was another early marriage problem. Thank God that in my family I had learned never to hit a woman. I remember in my teenage years, a girl hit me on the head with a brick. I didn't retaliate even then.

When I got angry with Joyce, I would walk out. But there was another exit strategy I kept considering – divorce. As I grew as a Christian, I realised how harmful it was to even entertain the thought of divorce. I sought help and ministry and by God's grace, anger left.

Philip's airline service

If you don't step out in faith, how can you expect a miracle? That's how Joyce and I found ourselves transported by the Holy Spirit. Let me explain.

Once we had moved out of the flat near St Mark's, we lived in a friend's flat in Catford. We had been invited by other friends to travel to Brixton to help with an open-air street event. The problem was, we only had enough money for a one-way trip on the bus. We still felt strongly to live in the way George Müller had, and not to ask people for money. But this presented us with a problem. How did we get home after the event?

'Never mind,' I said. 'God wants us there, He'll get us back. Maybe one of our friends will help.'

So off we went. The event was a success and we found ourselves back at a friend's house in Brixton. This friend had been very generous to us in the past and I was confident that she would provide the bus fare. Other friends came and went and as we approached 11pm, it became obvious that we were being asked to leave. The problem was our friend had not offered any money to us.

We said our farewells and began to walk. It was a chilly October night and it soon became obvious that neither of us had the right clothes on. We were getting cold. Added to that, Joyce was not wearing particularly sensible shoes and her feet were beginning to hurt after a couple of miles.

I actually had a £20 note in my wallet. But this had been given by another friend to purchase some audio equipment. I felt it would not be right to break into it. It was quite a test!

Maybe we should hitch a lift – we had done that before. But as we prayed about it, I sensed that the Holy Spirit was not wanting us to do that either.

We stopped in the street and prayed. I held Joyce close to me. We closed our eyes and asked God to intervene.

'Lord, You know we need to get home. We've stepped out in faith. Will you meet us in that faith and get us home tonight? Amen.'

As I opened my eyes, I expected that maybe a friend would drive by. But what I saw left me speechless. We were standing outside our house in Catford! God had physically transported us home.

Not having the greatest faith at that point, I ran down to the end of the street to check the road sign. Sure enough; we were home. There had been no sensation of flying or of any movement. One moment we were on the streets on the way back from Brixton. The next moment, we were outside our house.

We had read of such things happening in the Bible. Philip is supernaturally transported to Azotus, three miles from the sea, from having been in the middle of the desert.[9] We used to joke about God doing this and called it 'Philip's airline service'. But for this to happen to us felt remarkable. As we opened the door to the house, we were laughing in the Spirit, caught up in the wonder of God's miracle. We were overcome by God's wonders. We felt the power of the Holy Spirit upon us. We couldn't stop singing and praising God for what He had done. We had stepped out and God had stepped in.

The next day the post arrived. One of the letters was from our friend in Brixton. She had sent it before we had travelled over, but it had not arrived in time. Inside were two bus passes for the next month. I felt the Lord say to me, as I welled up in tears, that we would never be without money again. He had come through for us in the most amazing of ways. He was faithful. We could trust Him in everything.

Financial miracles

That promise has been tested over the years, but God has always come through. I remember one time reminding God of His promise as we had no money in the house. I felt Him prompt me to go upstairs and look in the top pocket of an old suit. There inside the pocket was a £50 note. I have no recollection of ever receiving it, or of knowing it was there.

Many financial miracles have followed. There was the time I found a £20 note in a tree. It was just up there, tucked in a branch.

---

9. See Acts 8:39-40.

It was winter, so with no leaves on the tree, the note was clearly visible. Another time I found a £20 note wrapped around my foot. On both occasions I had no money on me and the immediate need for God to provide. Often we would find just the amount we needed in the box at the back of the church building. And on many occasions we found money put through the letter box, meeting exact needs, with no note attached and with no idea who had posted it.

When we prayed the prayer 'Give us this day our daily bread',[10] we meant it. That was our daily prayer for financial miracles. We trusted God to provide. We would invite people around for meals, aware that God would have to provide as there was no food in the house. Again and again, He answered.

We had heard about a Dutch evangelist who had at one time shouted 'glory!' into his empty kitchen cupboards and seen them miraculously filled some time later. I came down to breakfast one morning to find Joyce doing the same. She explained that we were practically out of food and needed a miracle. Together we completed the round of kitchen cupboards, shouting 'glory' or 'hallelujah' into each one.

That same day, money arrived from three different sources. By the end of the day, we had been able to fill our cupboards.

We needed a short holiday at one point and on the way down to Gatwick Airport, stayed with our friends Michael and Jill Conrathe. We had the money to get to the airport the next day, but did not have the final payment on the tickets. Following our

10. Matthew 6:11, KJV.

usual model, we prayed about this, but did not say anything to our hosts.

Unbeknown to us, Michael had felt prompted to give an amount that would exactly meet the cost of the tickets. But, as we had been sharing through the evening about how God had met our needs, Michael began to have second thoughts.

'Jill,' he said to his wife. 'These guys are better provided for than we are. Perhaps I didn't hear God on this after all.'

But Jill was persistent.

'If God has said it, you should give it!'

He did. And we were able to take our holiday.

The apostle Paul writes to his friend and disciple Timothy, saying that even when we are without faith, God is faithful.[11] We have found it to be true.

I felt God tell me that Joyce and I had 'passed the test' that day we were transported. I don't think it is wrong to tell people of financial needs, but for us, as I said earlier, we felt to live as George Müller had done. Once you have made that decision, it's good to stick with it. Having the money in my pocket for the audio equipment and keeping true to the use for which it was given – not using it that night – was part of that test. We have stayed true to that way of living over the years, and have travelled the world, seeing miracles of all kinds, including financial ones. Sometimes we have served God seemingly without money, but He has always provided for us.

We have never been without.

---

11. See 2 Timothy 2:13.

Chapter Nine
One-way Ticket

Joyce and I had been praying about a second trip to Malaysia. They wanted us back, and we felt it right to go. But as usual, there would be a lot of praying as to how to get there!

The answer came courtesy of St Mark's. Our friends recognised the calling we had to Malaysia and arranged for a collection in order to get us there. There was more than enough for two return tickets, as well as living expenses. But we had felt God tell us to only buy one-way tickets. We figured that God would get us back as and when He wanted.

As we arrived at Heathrow, we had no idea that this adventure would last more than a year and involve trips to Singapore, the Philippines and Thailand as well as eight months in Malaysia.

We were developing a lifestyle of faith. Moving around. Preaching. Offerings covered our needs. Gifts were given. Cars were loaned. And God moved.

The east coast

Soon after arriving, we decided to travel up the east coast of Malaysia. This region was predominantly Muslim, with very little Christian witness. It seemed a good place to start. We met a number of Christians, many in difficult circumstances. We would encourage them in any way we could, stopping with them to pray and share the Word. One night, after an evening of interceding for local believers, I found myself sleeping on the floor – or not sleeping would be more accurate. I was uncomfortable and felt there was quite a battle in the heavenly places over the area we were staying in. So, I continued to pray through the night. There was a strong wind and the roof of the local mosque blew off. No one was hurt. We took it as a sign in the natural as to what God was doing in the spiritual realm. There is power in prayer.

We had heard of an Assemblies of God Pentecostal minister in the area, so we sought him out. Colin Hurt was a former principal of Mattersey Hall Bible college in the UK and had felt God call him to work in these Muslim areas. He had begun to establish a church in Kuantan and had been supernaturally led to a family of believers who had been waiting for someone to come to them and help establish a church. I had the privilege of helping Colin with those early meetings as the church grew.

This time was characterised by Joyce and I listening to God as to where to go and who to be with. One time we were invited to preach at a large church. I was excited, but then I felt the Lord telling me to say no to the invitation and instead to go to a small village. As we arrived in the village, we were welcomed by a family of believers and in particular by a nine-year-old girl who had heard of our time in Malaysia.

'It's my birthday today,' she said, 'and I prayed that you would come.'

I love that God hears the prayers of little children and puts them above the needs of big churches!

Miracles

Miracle followed miracle as we stepped out and learned to listen to the directions of the Holy Spirit. We worked with Joyce's uncle, Joy Sevaratnum. Joy was a doctor, but was not afraid to pray for miracles alongside his doctor's diagnosis. I prayed for a man in one of Dr Joy's meetings who had a cancerous growth on the side of his brain nearly as big as a football. As I placed my hand on him, every one of us saw the cancer shrink. There were many more miracles that night as our faith was stirred by what God had done. One of the most moving experiences was praying for a baby that had died. As we stood with the parents and laid hands on her head, there was a sudden cough and intake of breath as she was raised from the dead.

One miracle was of a different kind. We prayed for a young lady who had one leg quite a lot shorter than the other. Nothing happened, but she was positive that God would answer. She began to declare her healing, telling everyone God had done the work. The problem was, she was still limping. Her pastor asked us to intervene as she was embarrassing the church with her 'declaration'. We spoke to her, but she would not stop saying that God had healed her.

Sometime later, we were back in her church – and there she was, completely healed. Her persistence and continued declaration had been answered by God. I had to repent of my poor attitude towards her original declaration. God has many ways of answering us.

There were financial miracles in Malaysia too. Within the first three months, we had given most of the money from St Mark's away, and were trusting God for our living expenses. One day in a small village, I was chased by a lady. She was old and dressed in a faded black shawl. She pressed a substantial amount of money into my hand.

'I can't take this from you!' I said. 'You are poor yourself. I can't take it!'

'Young man,' she said. 'You cannot rob me of my blessing. Please take the money.' And with that, she started to cry.

Within a few moments, we were both in tears, as I gratefully accepted God's provision from this poor village lady. Living by faith can be a humbling experience.

Money and gifts came from all sorts of places. A church gave us a brand-new car to drive while we were there.

Singapore and the Philippines

As the time away rolled into the next decade, the 1980s, I felt stirred to travel down to Singapore. Situated on an island at the base of Malaysia, this sovereign city-state has a long history linked to the UK.

As usual, we went by faith. When the air fare arrived, we flew into the city, not knowing where we would go or how we were to serve – just that God had called us to be there. Reverend Nicholas gave us the name of the dean of the diocese of Singapore. Moses Tay gave us a warm welcome and opened up all the Anglican churches in the city to our ministry, including St Andrew's Cathedral where we were able to hold a number of meetings. Moses later became Bishop of Singapore and then Archbishop for South-East Asia.

I remember walking up the spiral steps of the pulpit at the cathedral and thinking what an amazing thing it was. Here was the borstal boy, the petty thief and drug-user preaching in the grandest of buildings. I smiled as I started to preach. God's sense of humour at work again.

Despite the grand surroundings and the largely middle class and comfortable congregation, many were brought to a living faith in Christ. The same was true of the other Anglican churches we were invited to.

Most of the time while I preached, Joyce would feel it was her job to intercede for me behind the scenes. While so necessary, especially when you are in a different environment, it was during our time in Singapore that I began to become uncomfortable with her just fulfilling that role.

'Joyce, I believe God has an upfront ministry for you as well.'

'Really? I'm not so sure!'

'I am! You may come over as shy, but there is such a faith in you. How about you beginning to preach as well? I really want to encourage you, Joyce. There's a ministry there!'

And so it was. That was the beginning of a lifetime of preaching and teaching for Joyce, alongside my own ministry. She regularly overcomes her fears and shyness and has developed a superb teaching ministry. In addition, she is a great mentor and has grown in confidence in this ministry. There are many that have lived with us over the years that are different today because of Joyce's input into their lives. I'm glad I listened to the whispers of the Holy Spirit in Singapore.

We saw many miracles during our visit. Numbers were healed.

Most exciting for us were the meetings in some of the schools. Canon James Wong accompanied us to the schools and we saw scores of children respond to the gospel message.

After nearly three months in Singapore I felt God tell me to go to the Philippines. This was a longer journey by air, around 1,500 miles. The cost would be considerable, and again, we had no accommodation or known contacts. Joyce struggled with my need to go there.

'It's not that I don't share your faith, David. I can see how God answers us. But why the Philippines? We don't know anyone there. And we can see God working with us here!'

I prayed.

Within a day, Joyce started to see all sorts of confirmations for our journey. There were posters advertising the Philippines that she hadn't noticed before. There were conversations with friends who mentioned the country. People passed her in the street and the Philippines was printed on their T-shirts! God had got her attention, and in the end she was telling me we *had* to go as she had no peace to stay!

'God will not leave me hungry'

There was a deeper work going on in Joyce at this time. She had accepted my living by faith, but because of her background and her struggle with poverty as a child, she had not entirely embraced the faith lifestyle. She decided to study the scriptures on financial giving but very quickly found the Holy Spirit prompting her to read more about God as our Father. Joyce came out of a deep study in the Bible completely transformed. She had met her

Father God in a new and deeper way and was able to say, 'God will not leave me hungry.' From that day on, Joyce has been as sharp as me, if not sharper, on living by faith.

As we touched down in Manila, the capital of the Philippines, we were both excited. God had spoken to us so clearly about coming here; what was He going to do? Canon James Wong had phoned ahead from Singapore and we were met at the airport by Canon Andrew. Driving a beaten-up old van that needed a screwdriver to open the doors, Andrew was to be our guide.

Within a few days, we were preaching in the cathedral and a number of other related churches. Through one visit to a church youth group, we were introduced to a girl in hospital. Unlike the UK health service, if you didn't have the money for an operation, you were effectively sent home to die. This girl needed an exploratory operation as a matter of urgency and we felt God telling us to pay for it. We had received the equivalent of nearly £3,000 from our work in Singapore – a substantial amount at the time, especially when we had no regular income. But we felt God telling us to give the money for the operation and trust Him for more. We did so.

It turned out that the girl had a burst appendix and had we delayed another day, she would have died. We had the thrill of seeing her back in the youth group within a few weeks.

But it did mean that once again we were virtually without money. In fact, we had just a few dollars for some grocery shopping.

The next day, Joyce was taken to the supermarket by some friends. Joyce was being very careful about what she spent, but the ladies with her kept putting more things in the supermarket trolley. Joyce would quietly take them out, knowing we didn't have the money for them. Laughing, the ladies put them back again! They explained that God had told them they were to buy the groceries for us. As Joyce had learned in her Bible study, God was not about to leave us hungry.

Meeting Michael

Our time in the Philippines did not go uncontested. At one time, the students of the local Catholic theological college threw stones at us. We weren't too keen to follow the apostle Paul in all his sufferings, so we made a hasty retreat. As they got to know us, the threats from the students lessened and they became aware that God was with us in the work we were doing.

God also introduced us to some wonderful people, many of whom are still friends today.

As we stepped out of the car in Baguio, a young man stood in front of us, casually dressed in T-shirt and shorts and with passion in his eyes.

'Hi, I'm Michael,' he said.

Michael Pangwi had been working as an Anglican missionary in the Philippine Episcopal Church for some years and had built a good-sized congregation in the city of Baguio. God had been using him a lot to heal people, but this had drawn him to the attention of the Episcopal Church hierarchy in Manila. As a result, Michael was about to be excommunicated for not following the more formal practices of the Church. As we arrived, this stand-off had been going on for a while. The congregation had advised the headquarters that if the Church were to remove Michael from his role, they would go with him – and more to the point, so would the building, which was not owned by the Episcopal Church. Michael was later to leave the denomination, but at that time, the warning from the congregation had been enough.

It's always been interesting to me to see how things are contested when God moves in power. Michael was seeing mighty miracles. In one meeting, twelve people received their hearing. All were 100 per cent healed. The blind saw, crippled people walked. The stories of the Bible were being re-enacted in front of us.

I saw a picture in the Spirit of Michael with thousands of fish being caught. Michael took this seriously and even put up a mobile on the ceiling of his study, with fish on it. Today the picture has become reality with around 5,000 people in Michael's home church and many churches planted around the world.

Our role with Michael was to help teach the Word. Many of those saved and receiving miracles were going out and ministering themselves. As a result, there were people in ministry who were just a few weeks old in their faith. This was great – except that they didn't know their Bible yet, so Joyce and I helped all we could with the training. The raw faith of our new recruits could almost be touched and felt. It made for an electric atmosphere. God's power was on display on a daily basis and many were being saved as a result.

Forty dollars

Returning to Malaysia from the Philippines proved to be a further test of our faith. Most of our money had gone to help the young lady in hospital and we only had $40 as we entered Malaysia. The country is strict on admittance and the granting of a visa. They ask you for proof of a return flight and that you have the finances you will need.

We were not too worried as we had a pastor friend collecting us from the airport who would be able to vouch for us. The only problem was, he wasn't there. As we sought visa approval for a further three months, my heart was pounding and both of us were praying in tongues under our breath. No money. No contact to verify accommodation. No return ticket.

The man at the desk looked at us quizzically, and then without a word, stamped our passports, granting a three-month visa. Not a word. Not a question.

In all the years of travelling into Malaysia, this is the only time we have not been asked for the usual proofs. What a God we serve.

We were puzzled by the non-arrival of our pastor friend, so we went to see him. It turned out that in our absence, there had been some gossip about us, which he had believed. He had therefore cancelled all of our preaching and teaching appointments without asking us and without checking the facts. The accusations were made up, of course.

We learned in one day how God provides and how the devil spoils.

Rivers and jungles

With all our meetings cancelled, we took the opportunity to work with a Methodist lady in the Malaysian jungles. It wasn't easy to get a permit to go, as there was an insurgent army in the jungle, as well as government troops trying to find them.

We drove a distance, and then began to walk. It was so hot, my clothes were soaking wet from perspiration. They stayed wet as we crossed a fast-flowing river – plenty more praying at that point! One of the girls with us got swept down the river, but was able to hold onto a tree branch and was rescued.

At the jungle village, some freshly caught fish was cooked for us; the taste, after nearly half a day walking in the jungle, was heavenly!

All the houses were on stilts, but there didn't seem to be too many people around. The man who had met us beckoned us to climb down and go to another part of the village. Upon arrival, he pointed to the corner of one of the buildings. Having climbed up, we found an elderly woman there. She was obviously bedridden, and we later found out that she had been unable to walk for around twenty years.

We didn't have that information at that point, though. With little in the way of translation, we prayed for the lady and instructed her to get up and walk.

She did.

This got the attention of the rest of the tribe. Soon enough, the biggest of the buildings was full and we were able to preach Christ.

At one point during the day, the monsoon rains arrived. The noise on the roof was so loud I had to stop preaching. At first, I wasn't sure what to do, but I decided that if Jesus could calm a storm,[12] I could stop the rain for the sake of His gospel.

---

12. See Mark 4:35-41.

I shouted: 'In Jesus' name, I command the rain to stop!'

Within a minute, the rain ceased and there was silence. Again, this got the attention of the rest of the village and we saw well over 100 people give their lives to Jesus Christ.

Before we returned through the jungle in the early evening (we only had a permit for a day), we prayed for the sick. Mighty miracles followed. People who had not walked for years, walked. A number of elderly blind people completely received their sight. A number of deaf people were healed. Others were delivered, including the son of the headman of the village who had been declaring himself to be the returned Jesus Christ.

As we walked back through the forest in the early evening, we were singing praises to our God, who in one day had saved a village and performed mighty miracles. We later learned that this one day was the catalyst for ongoing revival in the jungle areas.

A number of headmen from the different villages sought us out over the following month, asking us to come back. But we were never able to get another permit. The leader of the government troops in the area was amazed that we had received the first permit.

The revival went on for the next year or so. Most of the villages were reached and many hundreds of villagers found Jesus Christ to be real and life-changing. Hundreds were healed, many of significant conditions. Hundreds more were baptised in the Holy Spirit. The songs in the villages changed from local folk songs to worship songs. Children were praying for their parents. Families were travelling to long-lost relatives to tell them of Christ. It was a remarkable revival, all beginning with what was no more than a number of hours in the jungle that one day.

If the pastor hadn't believed the gossip, we would not have linked up with the Methodist missionary, and would never have gone into the jungle. In the Bible it says that what the enemy intends for harm, God intends for good.[13] We witnessed this to be true.

The navy base

Another friend had contacts in the Royal Malaysian Navy, so it wasn't long before we were preaching to the enlisted men at their naval base at Lumut. As the meeting went on, the third-highest-ranked naval officer on the base entered the meeting. All the sailors stood to attention and saluted. He quickly seated them again and invited us to continue.

At the end of my talk, I invited anyone who wanted to know Christ as their Saviour to come to the front of the room. One of the first to respond was the naval officer.

God reaches out to the unknown villagers in the jungle and to the senior officers in the navy. Everyone needs salvation.

---

13. See Genesis 50:20.

Chapter Ten
Home Adventures

Walking faithfully with God is an adventure. If we are obedient, there is nothing that God can't do. As we arrived back in the UK after a year away, we found God to be just as faithful. The miracles we witnessed in Malaysia and the Philippines were being repeated right back at St Mark's Church at the Kennington Oval.

The church had continued to grow while we were away. The less formal evening meetings were still going on past midnight on occasion. We were getting known as a place to visit. Christians were coming from many other churches and other backgrounds and denominations throughout London, and from further afield, to find out what it was that God was doing. The answer was, He was doing a lot! Our friend Rosie Virgo joined the church around this time. She was quite shy at first, but we saw in her the leadership potential that God had given her. Joyce began to disciple her and over time, Rosie became more confident and mature as a believer.

It was common to see miraculous healings. People would often be falling to the floor under the power of the Holy Spirit, and would stay there for hours. Many times, well after midnight, we would be helping those most powerfully touched by the Spirit to stand and walk out of the building.

It didn't need meetings for God to move, of course. One friend got baptised in the Spirit and started speaking in tongues in the bath! It was so easy to encounter the Holy Spirit. He was touching people right across the community, arresting them where they were, causing them to cry out to God and find salvation.

Healings and salvations

I remember one lady arriving for the evening meeting. Her hands were unnaturally twisted. She explained that she used to do a lot of knitting and even felt that this was a gift God had given her, in order to bless others. But now, with severe arthritis, she could no longer hold a knitting needle.

As we prayed, right in front of our eyes, her hands began to straighten. By the time she went home that night, she had been fully healed. The proof arrived a few weeks later when a knitted jumper arrived in the post!

One of the people regularly attending was a local school headmaster. There was a word of knowledge in a particular meeting about someone that God was miraculously healing from smoking. He smoked forty cigarettes a day at the time, but dismissed the word, deciding it was for someone else – and went outside for a smoke!

The next morning, he got up and made himself a coffee. It was his regular practice to make an early cup of coffee and have a smoke before the day started. He realised that on this occasion, he'd forgotten to light a cigarette. But the amazing thing was, he didn't want to light up. During the night, God had completely taken away his habit. The word had been for him. Even though he hadn't responded, God did the work anyway.

A Mauritian lady came to one of the meetings with an incurable illness. But not incurable to God. She was healed, had it confirmed by the doctors, and went on to tell the rest of the family about what God had done. This resulted in seventeen members of her family, some of them Muslims, coming to Christ. One of them was her son, Linley. He had been running with the gangs in east London. One night during his days with the gangs, he lifted a hammer to hit someone on the head, but the hammer slipped from his grasp despite, as he put it, having had a tight grip on it. He realised that this was God getting his attention. Linley had actually prayed to God a while before, effectively saying, 'If You heal my mum, I will serve You.' And here was Mum speaking of God's healing. He gave his life to Christ.

It was a concern to the Mauritian lady that her husband had not responded to Christ. Shortly after, he had a serious heart attack and ended up in hospital. As he regained consciousness, there was a nurse there who spoke of Christ and led him to faith. God had dealt with the whole family.

Every night we were seeing miraculous healings. Cancers gone. Legs straightened. Back vertebrae clicking into place. Skin conditions healed in front of our eyes. Deaf ears opened. Eyes healed. Miracle after miracle. It was almost a daily event. Everything we had dreamed of was happening in front of us. We were disappointed when something *didn't* happen.

The people being healed attracted many without a faith to come and observe. But God has a way of working and it was a rare thing for someone without a faith in Christ to go home that night still unsaved. There were people from every kind of background – some of those in the parish who had been church stalwarts for years found that the faith they had had been in religion. They were wonderfully set free from religion, finding a living faith in Jesus. Others were straight off the streets, the forgotten of society, lost and alone. So many turned their life around in those meetings, finding a faith and a reason to live again.

God used wonderful ways in getting people to the meetings. One night there was a bomb scare in the area, so at 3am, Reverend Nicholas opened up the church building to shelter people and offer them tea and coffee. The church got such a good reputation from the locals for doing this that many then turned up at the church meetings – and got saved.

At the time, there were a lot of burglaries going on in the neighbourhood. Some of the perpetrators turned up at the meetings. We actually challenged them. We said that the church building and the vicarage were protected by God and His angels, and they wouldn't be able to get in and burgle them. One young lad spoke of his brother coming out of prison and assured us that his brother would be successful. He did try – but God protected. The vicarage ended up being the only house on the whole street that wasn't burgled.

The team

One morning I was on my face in my lounge, praying and crying out to God. God spoke to me that morning in an audible voice. He said: 'Man of God, get up off your face. Take the people over the Jordan.'

I had such an inferiority complex in those days! Just to hear the phrase 'man of God' was good for me. When I heard the word, I looked around for the man of God, before realising it must be me He was talking to as I was the only one there! The rest of the sentence made complete sense too. I had been considering forming a team and taking them out on the streets, rather than just waiting for people to turn up at the meetings. I needed to take them over the metaphorical Jordan River and out of their comfort zone.

I responded to the challenge and over the next few weeks, a team went out to the shopping centres on a regular basis, worshipping in the open air and praying for healings. We again saw many answered prayers and miraculous healings. I would always preach the gospel as well and numbers were saved and added to St Mark's.

A young man who came out with us began to surreptitiously take over the team. He would arrange times when we couldn't go ourselves, and hold additional meetings before and after the outreaches. It bothered us a bit, as we weren't sure of his motives. Reverend Nicholas told us not to worry. He reminded us of the story in Numbers chapter 17 in the Old Testament, of Aaron's rod budding. This was God's way of showing He was with Aaron at a time of challenge. We accepted the advice and left things as they were.

A month or so later, the young man came back to us and invited us to take over the team again as he felt he had finished his ministry there. What he didn't tell us was that there was practically no team left – people has simply stopped coming. The moment we took the team back on, the people from St Mark's came back and we saw many more months of productive ministry on the streets.

The bomb scare and the church responding to it had given us a 'God key' when we were on the streets. There had been so many burglaries in the area that were someone to call at one of the houses, often the owner was afraid to open the door. But when some of my team went door-to-door to tell people about Christ, doors were opened. The moment we said we were from St Mark's, neighbours would open their doors and welcome us in.

One lady asked us into her home. She had a baby in her arms. There was a significant growth on the baby's head. I felt we had to offer to pray.

'We're Christians. We believe God can heal. Would you allow us to pray for your baby?'

We laid our hands on the baby's head, and there in front of us, the growth disappeared. Needless to say, the mum was at church that Sunday and got wonderfully saved.

Changed lives

At the time, there were many remarkable stories of changed lives.

A number of our Malaysian friends were visiting the UK during this time, and they often stayed with us. One was Dorothy, a staunch Buddhist. It wasn't long, though, before she was surrendering her life to Christ at the end of one of the meetings.

Amit came to stay with us too. He was a Hindu and had travelled to the UK in pursuit of his wife, who was a former neighbour of Joyce's from her time in Malaysia. The problem was that his wife didn't want anything to do with him due to the way he had treated her. Amit was depressed. Joyce caught him on more than one occasion in our house, trying to take his life. We decided we had to do something.

I sat Amit down and talked to him about our faith. Nothing too strong, but enough to get his interest. I gave him a Bible and suggested he read it. I said to him that it was a 'storybook' that would interest him.

Not long after, Amit came to a church meeting and prayed a prayer to ask Jesus into his life. Later that same morning, he came over to me.

'That's a funny storybook, David. It speaks to you!'

It seems that as Amit had read the Bible, God had already started a work in him so that, full of Bible stories, he came to the church meeting already prepared by God's Holy Spirit.

Dorothy and Amit were both discipled by us over the next months as they stayed with us, and to this day, as far as we are aware, are continuing with their Christian journey.

Hakim was another person through our doors. A Lebanese refugee, he had fled from a plot on his life and given up a lucrative business, escaping to England. Hakim was a Muslim and it was a slow journey for him to learn, understand and respond to Christ. But respond he did. As he began to communicate his change of faith to his family in Lebanon, word reached him that the family had held a 'funeral' for him, considering him dead to them because of his Christian conversion.

Danny appeared on our doorstep at three in the morning, complete with suitcase. He was of a Roman Catholic background and when his mother heard of his conversion, she threw him out. He was a bricklayer and hated his job. But as God continued to work in Danny's life, and to change him, Danny began to appreciate that what he was doing was working for the Lord, in accordance with Paul's letter to the Colossians in the Bible.[14] This transformed him. And his best building work followed this transformation.

Dil was a converted Hindu. He wasn't so good at leading people to a faith in Christ, but he was great at gathering them. He once managed to collect nearly fifty escaped Polish sailors (during the Communist era) and deliver them to church where they heard the gospel and were saved.

A young student called Andrew White arrived at the church and quickly gave his life to Christ. It is a privilege to have played a small part in his life story, which later saw him working in harrowing conditions as the Vicar of Baghdad.

Gerry was a pickpocket with a stall on Petticoat Lane. He came into a meeting once, because he liked the rather clever posters that the vicar had put up. By the end of the meeting, he had repented of his lifestyle and went home to tell the Bunny Girl he was living with that he had to leave her because Jesus Christ had changed his life. She was surprised by the obvious change in him, and came along to St Mark's as well. This resulted in her salvation, their marriage and a large and happy family in future years.

Gerry later became ill with leukaemia. He sadly died, but not before he had led most of the hospital ward to Christ.

---

14. See Colossians 3:23.

Chapter Eleven
Fighting for Family

It was during our time at St Mark's that we began to see some of my family express an interest in our faith. We had been fighting in prayer for our family to come to faith in Christ. And one of the first encounters was nearly a literal fight.

'I don't fight any more'

My former brother-in-law Jack (he had once been married to Irene) turned up one night. He was drunk, living in a car and spoiling for a fight. As he tried to grapple with me at the door to our flat, I said to him, 'I don't fight any more.' Jack stepped back, a look of confusion on his face. He was drunk and drugged up. I commanded the demonic spirits to leave him. As he stood there, I saw them drain out of his feet. He had felt it too and looked astounded.

Gerry was still on the scene at that time and over the next few months, took time with Jack to lead him to a faith and help him get free from drink and drugs. I remember at least one occasion when Gerry rescued me during a church service when Jack had regressed and had come to the meeting to harm me. As Gerry 'bounced' him out of the church building, a knife fell from Jack's coat.

The first but not the last

I regularly prayed for my family – especially over a two-year period soon after my own conversion. I even wrote up a family tree on a piece of paper that Joyce and I would pray over. I heard God tell me that I wasn't to worry about my family, that God was on the case and that He had heard my prayers. God told me not to try to 'save them' but that He would do so. God told me to 'act like a son' and not like Billy Graham! This brought a lot of comfort to me.

It's funny. With a surname of 'Lamb', I used to joke I was the black sheep of the family. But of course, I became whiter than white through Christ. Living like that in front of the family was hard. They knew the 'black sheep' days and would regularly remind me of them.

I would meet most of the family every Christmas and I was usually the target for religious jokes because of my faith, especially as they got more and more drunk on Christmas Day. I put up with it, continuing to pray for each of them.

My sister Grace was the first. Along with her husband, Wallace, she started attending a Newfrontiers church and it was a delight to see them both continue to grow in their faith. However, Grace struggled with some mental health problems and stopped attending church. It was later the same year that I heard Grace had been admitted to hospital and wasn't expected to live. She had suffered a severe brain aneurism. I immediately went to see her, and prayed over her while she was unconscious. While I was there, an African church with a connection to friends of ours decided to pray through the night for Grace. I was advised by a nurse that things didn't look good and that most patients with this condition did not survive. I continued to pray, asking God to bring her back.

The next day I called again, to see Grace awake and wanting to give me a hug. As I hugged her, she whispered in my ear, 'I'm back!' It was meant not only to refer to her medical condition, but to her spiritual one too. Not long afterwards, with Grace fully recovered, I had the privilege of baptising her.

There was someone looking on during this season; Grace and Wallace's son Gerald. He was fifteen years old at the time. I spoke to him about Christ on a number of occasions, but there was little interest.

'Uncle, you've seen the world. I want to as well! I'm not going to look at any belief. Don't talk to me about your religion – and stop giving me those books! I want to travel.'

We lost touch for a short while and when I next saw Gerald, he was a lot bigger. A giant of a man, someone who clearly worked out in the gym, he was an imposing figure. By then, he was working as a window cleaner – something I had taught him.

Fast forward to 2010. I was leading a service in Ashford, Kent, when a man entered the church. He was bigger again than I remembered and had put on a lot of weight, but there was no missing who it was. Gerald sat at the back and gave me a wave.

Near the end of the service, there was a word of knowledge that God wanted to heal someone with gout. Two people responded and both were healed. One of them was Gerald. I gave him a 'Bridge to Life' booklet explaining Christian salvation and said I'd be in touch with him.

In fact, I didn't have to wait that long. Two days later, I got a call from Gerald's wife, Jackie, asking what I had done to him.

'What do you mean, what have I done?'

'Well, he's just so happy. His anger has gone. He's stopped drinking. And his gout has gone. He's read right through the New Testament and he's laughing all the time. What did you do? Whatever it is, I want it too!'

It wasn't long before a slimmed-down Gerald was hitting the streets, praying for people to be healed. In Gerald, I have found a family member to stand with me. Some of the older folks in the family were near to death and it has been a privilege to regularly pray along with Gerald for their salvation. I may have been the first in my family to be saved, but I am not the last.

More family

As the years have gone by, I have had the privilege of seeing more of my family find a faith in Christ. Uncle Billy, my dad's older brother, found Christ after talking to Joyce and me, just a few weeks before he died. Uncle Ray, dad's youngest brother, who lived in Toronto, came to Christ as I spoke with him, following a miraculous plane ticket that got me out there.

My favourite auntie was always Auntie Bella. It was Auntie Bella who lived upstairs from me when I was a young boy. I had spent many happy hours with her. We even took her to a Louis Palau gospel crusade in her early eighties. At the end of the evening, I asked her if she wanted to go forward.

'No, I'm not ready, David.'

'Auntie, how old are you?'

'I'm eighty-three. '

'Auntie, when *will* you be ready?!'

At the age of eighty-six, with my auntie now living in a care home in Acton, which was managed by nuns, I was able to lead her to a faith in Christ. That was especially precious for me.

My mum's sister, Auntie Ginny, lived in Fulham. She could be hard work, with every other word a swear word. She had cancer and I managed to get her into the same hospital I was working in at the time. I had been given a brief at this hospital to look after the older patients, and was working more as a chaplain than a nurse. It was a privilege to bring Auntie Ginny to Christ.

The next day, I got a visit from my cousin; Ginny's daughter.

'What have you done, David?'

'What do you mean?'

'What have you done to my mum? This is the first day in my life when she hasn't cursed me.'

Others in my family are on a journey. But what I have noticed is a softening towards me and to the Christian faith. Probably the most resistant to the gospel was my sister Irene's second husband, Roy. He'd been one of those most often in trouble with the law in our earlier years, and was now living out in the States. I was amazed when a message reached me from Roy to tell me that he'd been born again. You never know, when you sow the seed, what the results will be.

Mum and Dad

Needless to say, I regularly prayed for my parents to come to Christ. I had God's word that I was to act as a son and not as a mad evangelist, so I had prayed a lot but not preached at them.

It was during my two years at Jean and Elmer Darnall's Bible school, while I was living at home, that Mum's life changed. One morning she brought me a cup of tea in bed.

'David, I wonder whether I could come with you to that meeting you are speaking at?'

'Of course, Mum!'

This was a home meeting at Jimmy and Fynvola James' house in Northwood. Mum came along. She was pretty quiet during the meeting but I heard her talking to Dad when we got home.

'Our David speaks really well, you know. And people tell stories – they call them testimonies. There must be a lot of people depressed, though; there was a lot of crying!'

Soon after, Mum and I were out walking.

'Tell me, David, what's all that "ching chung kung fu" stuff at the meeting?'

'Oh, that. That's a heavenly language that God can give you. It's a way of speaking to God when you run out of English words to say.'

'Oh, is that what it is?'

She seemed happy to accept my explanation.

Just a couple of weeks later at home, I had the privilege of praying with her and leading her to a faith in Christ.

For Dad, it was a longer journey. He was open to the possibility of there being a God, and on a number of occasions had recommended that his friends should 'come and talk to my David' when they were struggling with life.

I'd tried to talk to Dad about my faith numerous times. Too many of them were when Dad had had a drink or two and this fuelled arguments. Mum had rescued me on more than one occasion from an argument meltdown!

Some years after Mum's conversion, Dad was walking down a street near home. There was a young girl giving out Christian tracts. As Dad got near to her, an older woman started to shout at the girl, telling her to go, and to stop her 'Jesus bashing'. Dad came to the girl's defence. He stopped the lady from verbally abusing the girl and said that we lived in a country where there was free speech, so the girl should be able to do what she was doing.

When the lady went away, the girl came over to Dad to thank him for his intervention.

'Do you mind,' she said, 'if I just take you through what the tract says?'

'OK,' said Dad.

And there on the street, she explained the gospel to Dad. He had heard it before. He'd been in a Salvation Army brass band. He'd listened to me over the years – even been to some of my meetings. But that day, God broke in.

Back home, Dad was excited.

'David! It says here that we are all sinners. That we all need Jesus!'

I'd been telling him for years, of course. But the Holy Spirit was at work. Dad's eyes had been opened.

In 1989, I took Dad with me to see Billy Graham in London. And there, on a rainy night, he walked forward, through the puddles, to stand at the front and give his life to Christ. I was soaked by the rain. And my tears were washed away.

Chapter Twelve
Training for the Nations

'I don't want you to go, but God has spoken to me.'

I was in Reverend Nicholas' study. The week before I had asked him whether he thought Joyce and I could do with more training. That's certainly what we had been thinking. We had come onto staff at St Mark's and had been there, interspersed with mission trips, for nearly six years. It was a long time. And the longer we served, the more we felt the limitations of our own abilities. We relied on the Holy Spirit. But to receive training as well would be worthwhile.

Nicholas had originally tried to talk us out of it, as he knew it might mean us leaving, at least for a season. But a week later, he had heard from God. The decision was made; an offering was taken.

Colin Urquhart had been a regular visitor to St Mark's. Originally an Anglican himself, he had been greatly used in the charismatic renewal in the late 1970s and early 1980s. He had set up Kingdom Faith, his own ministry and Bible school in Sussex, and Joyce and I were to be some of the first students on what was a seven-month course. Our good friend Rosie Virgo also decided to join the programme.

Bob Gordon was the college principal and we benefited greatly from both his and Colin's teaching. The course was run on a 'by faith' basis, so all thirty students were regularly praying for enough income for themselves and for the college, to pay for the bills, food and upkeep.

Carpet sessions

Colin's teaching had a revival dynamic to it, and as students, we would regularly take what we had learned during the week out to churches at the weekend.

Alongside the teaching, one of Colin's emphases was to spend time with God, listening to Him. We had many times in what were called 'carpet sessions'. These were gatherings when we would often be flat out on the floor, seeking God, listening to the Holy Spirit, eager to hear His word and His direction over our lives. Sometimes these carpet sessions could go on through the night. After the full-on healing and evangelism work at St Mark's it took a bit of getting used to but, looking back, these became precious times of God's ministry into our lives and preparation for what was to follow.

God was dealing with me in another way as well. I was in my late thirties by now. I had been mightily used by God and perhaps I expected that God would continue to use me in this way. I expected Colin and the team to see it. But instead, I was simply part of a team, led by an (in my view) inexperienced and youthful leader. It was pride, of course, and before the training was over, I had to repent on more than one occasion!

That time with Colin and the team was so precious. We learned about revival. We cried out for revival. We had learned better how to listen to the whispers of the Holy Spirit. We had slowed down after the hectic ministry of St Mark's and we came away changed.

Cuckfield

At the end of the seven months, Joyce and I knew it was time to move on – but what to? Our friend Rosie felt the same and the three of us booked ourselves into the Youth With A Mission (YWAM) headquarters in Cuckfield in Sussex to fast and pray for a few days.

We walked out into the woods one afternoon to pray. Joyce and Rosie went on ahead and I walked slowly, kicking the ground, pondering what God was doing with each of us, crying out to Him for clear guidance. I could just see Rosie's blonde hair through the trees and Joyce with her, the smaller of the two, her black hair being blown back in the breeze. In the distance was a man walking towards them. I recognised him immediately. Oliver Nyumbu had led a mission at St Mark's, and was now one of the YWAM directors. I ran to catch up. As we sat in the woods, Oliver began to speak of YWAM and within a few minutes, our questions were answered – we knew for sure the direction God was taking us.

Oliver arranged for all three of us to go as trainee leaders to the main YWAM base near Nuneaton. It was a rich time for us; training on the YWAM Discipleship Training School, linked to weekend outreaches in Nottingham. In Nottingham we worked with local churches and put on a street drama called 'The Toy Maker'. The drama attracted hundreds of people and at the end we were able to preach and lead many to Christ.

On one occasion, working with an Anglican church in Nottingham, we experienced a particularly 'visual' healing. Frank had a leg that was considerably shorter than the other. He walked with a pronounced limp. We prayed for him as a team, and in front of our eyes, his short leg grew to the length of the other one. We all saw it happen. Frank ended the evening running around the church building with no sign of any discomfort or limp.

In addition to our Nottingham trips, Joyce, Rosie and I used to gather any volunteer YWAMers we could find and go out into local towns and villages to evangelise. During those early days of 1984, we had no idea we would still be with YWAM six years later.

Copenhagen

The end of the training saw us joining a mission in Copenhagen, the capital of Denmark, for a month. In typical YWAM style, we were not going to go to the easier tourist spots, but to areas shunned by others on mission. One place was known as the Black Square. The Black Square was an area of Nørrebro in Copenhagen where social unrest began to build in the 1970s and the police had been frequently required. By the time we were there, things had begun to calm down, but it still had a reputation that meant more 'sensible' missions would stay away!

I was preaching in the Black Square on one occasion when a lady arrived. She was known in the area and liked by the residents, but was slightly mad, and more to the point, operated as a witch. As I preached, she started to shout at me, eventually grabbing me around the throat. I continued to preach with this witch on my back. It was one of my more surreal moments in serving the Lord. I'm not sure who remembers what I preached (I don't), but everyone remembers the witch on my back.

Later on, we arranged for some children's singing there and it was interesting to note that this stopped the lady from operating. It seemed as if God had formed an invisible barrier around the children and the witch couldn't penetrate it. It's a reflection of the purity of spirit that is often in our children – plus a good deal of God's protection.

God gave us a word that no one would be harmed in our visits to the Black Square, and He kept us safe. But there were many times when we needed to remind God of that! Once a man advanced on us with a bottle above his head, telling us he was a Viking and if we didn't go he would kill us. We didn't go – and he didn't kill us. It seemed to us that those with demons manifesting in them somehow knew who the mission team leader was, and it was no surprise to us that he was the one to face the first attacks each day we were out on the streets.

While there was a lot of wilder activity on the streets, Joyce and Rosie were invited to speak to a more sedate ladies church group. Joyce had been spending a lot of time with God, getting healed of some past hurts, so by the time of the meeting, she was quite a powerhouse for the Holy Spirit. As the meeting began, Joyce's ministry spoke powerfully to the women. Most were in tears, many sobbing on the floor. The teaching and ministry were such that some of the women left to go and fetch other women. It was a day that revolutionised this group of faithful women.

Christiania

If the Black Square was tough, we were to see more yet. With the direction of our leaders, Mike and Jenny Jones, we went into the Freetown area of Copenhagen known as Christiania. This had started as a social experiment in the early 1970s when a former military area was taken over by squatters. The local council allowed it to continue and it became known as an area popularised by residents who were into Eastern meditation and yoga, together with a great deal of cannabis-smoking – all with a blind eye from the government. By the time we went there, things had got darker. The place had been taken over by gangs and the drug abuse had gone far beyond cannabis.

At the time we arrived, we had been studying Luke chapter 10 in the Bible. This is where Jesus talks about finding people of peace wherever we go. We prayed in the same way as we entered the gates of Christiania. Instead of being greeted by gang members as we had been told to expect, we were greeted by a member of the Christiania management committee. He introduced himself, and having understood who we were, became very excited. He had asked God to reveal Himself some months before. He had expected maybe to meet Buddha or some other deity as a result of his drug-induced prayer, but instead, a Roman Catholic priest came through the gates and announced to the man that God had sent him. So, upon our arrival, we had met up with the only known Christian on the main Christiania committee!

As we started to preach and sing, a crowd gathered. The clouds were heavy, but the rain held off. Beyond the crowd, there were many hanging out of the concrete jungle of flats above us. The crowd were fairly boisterous but most were listening and we found quickly that there was a rough kind of justice that they each followed. At one point, when a man was about to hit the speaker with a bottle, a young man stepped out of the crowd and hit him instead. With blood dripping from his nose, the original assailant ran away.

Later still, I was talking to two of the drug pushers, but their colleagues were not happy as I was stopping their trade. They set a dog on me. The first I knew about it was when I looked down and saw a bulldog tearing away the bottom part of my trousers. I shouted, 'In Jesus' name, I rebuke you!'

The same young man who had dealt with the man with the bottle came over, picked the dog up, and threw it into some bushes.

The young man looked at me. In good English he said, 'Tell me, sir, why do you get the devil to do the Lord's work?'

God gave me the words to say.

'I don't see you as the devil's servant at all. I see you as sent by God. Each time we have had a need for protection, you have shown up and dealt with it for us. It's God you're serving.'

We had a long chat after that which included the revelation that he was the youngest bank robber in the history of Denmark.

Not only did we meet the man of peace coming into Christiania, but then we had the man of protection as well! It was a wild day, but it saw many genuine salvations in among this seemingly lawless and drug-affected community.

Chapter Thirteen
To the World

After our training and time in Denmark, Joyce and I were given leadership of various evangelistic teams. This included an extended trip of five months to the Far East, including time in Malaysia, Singapore and Indonesia. The highlight of that trip, though, was definitely a visit to the Philippines. Joyce and I had been there before, of course, but this time we had a team of eight YWAMers with us, including Rosie.

The Holy Ghost Extension

The majority of our time there was up in an area called the Holy Ghost Extension. This is an administrative area within the Philippines, and despite its name, which has a Roman Catholic origin, the area was one of the most lawless districts in the country. Rebels hid in the region, and it was not safe to go anywhere after dark.

But we were excited. Just before we entered that region, God had prepared us. He had reminded us that it is always His agenda we follow and not our own.

We had a meeting in a church building where it's fair to say God showed up. He did so by way of an audible wind. The wind blew through the building and all of us were aware that it was a holy moment. There were around 1,000 people in the meeting and nearly every one of us fell on our faces. We couldn't move; we were so aware of the Holy Spirit's presence. The wind lasted for around twenty minutes and during that time many were healed, with many delivered from the demonic, including a witchdoctor.

As the Spirit lifted, I tried to carry on with the meeting. But it was impossible. We had been in His presence. He had brought His agenda. All we could do was stay silent, sit down and let God continue to minister.

As we drove into the Holy Ghost Extension, we knew God was going to move. We knew that the *real* Holy Spirit was about to do things in this lawless area that would change lives. All ten of us on the team were aware that God had taken things to a new level. Every one of us felt the close presence of the Spirit, thanks to the meeting, and we knew God was about to use us.

We took over a church for a couple of months while the pastor was away. Immediately, people started turning up for prayer. Word got around that our kind of prayers got answered! We didn't need to arrange meetings – people just came. Mothers would come during the day, youth in the evening. Men came sometimes and slept on the floor. We had to fumigate the building for fleas a few times because of that!

Many were finding a genuine faith in Christ, far removed from the legalistic religion they had been used to.

Our old friend from our earlier visit and now a vicar in one of the nearby cities, Michael Pangwi, was a particular encouragement to us. During one meeting, he was blessing new-born babies. One baby was handed to him by its mother. What she knew, and Michael didn't, was that the baby had died soon after birth. As Michael took the lifeless body and prayed God's blessing, there was a sudden cry from within the blanket. God had raised the baby from the dead.

God's calling card

Things became even more hectic in the Holy Ghost Extension when a lady was healed. She came to us during the day, bent over almost double. My interpreter wasn't there at the time, so I was not able to talk to her. Instead, I gathered the team around to pray. As we laid hands on her, the miracle happened. She completely straightened up. We later learned that God also healed her of other illnesses at that moment. She had been bent over for years. Locals called it the 'spirit of the mountains' to be afflicted in that way. I remember her to this day, running around the church building, shouting and praising God for her healing. It was not hard to lead her to a living faith in Christ after that.

It turned out that these kinds of miracles became God's calling card for the locals. He showed up in power, people got healed and as a result, many got saved.

The next day, the same lady returned, bringing with her another lady bent over with the same affliction. Again, God healed.

We used the opportunity afforded by this news, which quickly spread, to visit those in the houses around. The team led many to Christ over the breakfast and dinner table as we called on these local families.

Night-time provision

Joyce and I, with some of the team, had been visiting Michael Pangwi in the nearby city. But we had lost track of the time, and when we were ready to leave, night had fallen. It had been impressed on us by the YWAM leadership at the beginning of our trip that at no time should we be out in the Holy Ghost Extension after dark. YWAM had previously had two of their team martyred in this region.

But what were we to do? We couldn't stay with Michael, so we decided to try to find a taxi that would take us. That wasn't so easy. When the taxi drivers heard where we wanted to go, they simply refused to take us. Eventually we found a driver who was willing.

As we reached our accommodation, we saw a crowd of people running towards us. There was just time for a quick prayer before the crowd reached us. But it wasn't us they wanted; it was the taxi. A sniper had just shot the leader of the rebel opposition at a meeting in the village hall. Because we were there, the taxi was able to get him to hospital and his life was saved. We weren't allowed to speak with him, but we did manage to get help to his wife, and to pray with her.

As we left that area at the end of our two months with them, the whole village came out to say goodbye to the ten of us. Many were in tears. There was not a family left who did not have at least one person saved. Most were actively witnessing their faith, many of them copying us, the team and Michael in the way we prayed for people, and seeing the same supernatural results. The place had been transformed.

It was an excited team that came back from that trip. Over the years, Joyce and I have returned to the Philippines around a dozen times. We have continued to work with Michael, and are grateful for the way God has used us in that incredible country.

Birmingham

Other missions followed with YWAM. Joyce and I led teams to India, Sri Lanka, Kenya and then further trips to the Far East. The pace was relentless. I didn't notice at first, but I was slowly becoming worn down by it.

One of our biggest challenges turned out to be on home soil.

It was Oliver Nyumbu on the phone.

'David, please would you and Joyce pray about this? We're setting up a new unit in Birmingham to reach the Muslim community. We're starting with a team of 100 and after the initial push, we're going to keep a small team there. I'd like you guys to consider leading the evangelism part of the initiative.'

So it was we found ourselves living in Birmingham for the next three and a half years.

Initially it was chaotic. Looking after a team of 100 YWAMers each day was hard work. Joyce, with Rosie's help, undertook the logistics of feeding them while I led out the teams to areas of Birmingham where there were the greatest number of Muslims. These also tended to be some of the poorer areas where there was a high recorded rate of domestic violence and a subculture of gangs and knife crime.

We started leading outreaches in the parks and nearby shopping centres. We always started with a time of worship. There is something about worship that challenges those who don't have a Christian faith. A large number of young Muslim men would gather and start to throw stones at us. Small ones at first, but if we didn't move on, larger rocks came our way. This was accompanied by a considerable amount of verbal abuse. We had to be strong to stay the course.

One young man hanging around on the fringes of the Muslim gangs had a severe eye problem. His eyes were badly crossed. One of the team called him forward and began to pray for him. There, in front of everybody, the young man's eyes uncrossed and he received normal sight. The young men in the Muslim gangs saw this and didn't know what to do. In fact, if anything, the persecution increased after this healing.

One day an older Muslim man was looking on. He appeared to have severe back problems and was walking with a stick to help him. He stayed for a while watching the worship. There were a good many on the team that day, so the songs were loud.

Suddenly, the older man came forward, dropped his walking stick and knelt in front of us, joining in the worship as best he knew how. He stayed like this for a while and when he eventually got off his knees, we prayed for his back. It was instantly healed.

The man went to the mosque to tell the leaders there what had happened to him. The response was disappointing as they began to hurl insults at the man and tell him he was disobeying Allah.

I had a knife pulled on me in one of the parks one day. The young man looked me in the eye. I smiled. The man said, 'I just wanted to see how you would react,' and put the knife away.

It was hard to keep going to these areas and a number of the team were injured with the small stones that were thrown. But we noticed something else as well. The atmosphere began to change. What had appeared to us to be a feeling of darkness over the area, began to shift. Some of the shopkeepers started to welcome us. We began to get comments on the street as to how the shoppers were looking forward to us coming, how they enjoyed the music. The initial frowns from the locals changed to smiles.

On their level

I spent time on my own, praying and asking God to show me how to break into these communities, especially with the young men who remained aggressive. I felt the Lord tell me to use football as a way to engage them. It was a word of wisdom. The moment we started to play football with them, everything broke. All the hostility drained away. The young men began to listen.

We learned a lot on that mission. If we listened to them, they (or most of them) would listen to us. If we could get on their level with their interests, they listened. If we spoke of God speaking to us, they listened. If we saw miracles, they listened. If we showed genuine love, they listened.

The initial team of 100 were linked to a mission led by Nick Cuthbert, an evangelist and later, founder of Riverside Church, Birmingham. Once they left, we settled back into a time of smaller teams. Around eight of us lived in Birmingham, but we didn't just focus on that city. Over the next three years, we moved around the UK in our trusty seven-seater Peugeot, sponsored by a businessman. From Cornwall in the south through to the north of Scotland, we shared our faith through preaching and drama. We looked to God to heal, which often opened up conversations and conversions. Among the many healings we witnessed, a man with curvature of the spine was healed – this was later medically verified. In Nottingham, we saw God work by his Holy Spirit on a young girl, whose leg grew in front of us by at least an inch and a half.

Holy Spirit mayhem

As a team, we arranged to show a number of Christian-related films at a local cinema. I remember one in particular. Whether it was coincidence or deliberate, I'm not sure, but one night, two rival gangs showed up. They were messing around and taunting each other, not really paying much attention to the film.

The team got praying. We asked for such a move of the Holy Spirit that there could not possibly be any fighting.

The prayers didn't seem to work at first. The gangs began to square up to each other and started trading punches. They moved out of the cinema, into the atrium, and some out onto the street. We continued to pray.

As I ventured out, an amazing sight awaited me. God the Holy Spirit had come down on the two gangs. They were all on the ground. Some were draped over walls, others were on the pavement outside. All of them unable to fight; all of them on the ground, sensing the power of the Holy Spirit; most of them not aware as to what it was they were feeling.

We began to minister to them. It was mayhem, as demons were coming out of some of them. Some frothed at the mouth and gagged as God set them free.

When the police turned up expecting trouble, they looked flummoxed. We assured them that everything was under control and that there would be no problems there that night. The police watched as the rival gangs crawled to their knees, many of them dazed; almost 'drunk' with God's Spirit. Some had been out on the ground for thirty or forty minutes. They had no desire now for fighting, as the team witnessed to them and led some to Christ.

We were thrilled with all God was doing with the Birmingham team. In the middle of our time in Birmingham, I fitted in a YWAM trip to India where, again, there were many miracles.

The pace was hectic. And something was wrong. I had started to feel tired months earlier. Now I began to feel as if I was running on empty.

Exhaustion

The pace of life with YWAM had become too much for me. While in India, I began to feel exhausted. Back home, Joyce was struggling. She had a detached retina and had suffered two miscarriages and an ectopic pregnancy in the two previous years. As I looked at a family walking down the street, all holding hands, I cried out for our own childless situation.

God spoke to me at that moment. He reminded me that despite the perceived happiness of the family I was looking at that day in India, they were without Christ. I was reminded of all we had in Him. Of how God had protected us so many times. On that dusty street in India, the tears began to flow and I quietly worshipped.

Despite that moment, as I arrived back in Birmingham, I knew something wasn't right. I couldn't think straight. I didn't want to do anything. My body felt tired all the time. Joyce had to prompt me to eat. Thankfully the YWAM leaders recognised that they needed to do something and we found ourselves in a farmhouse a mile or so away from the YWAM Nuneaton base.

We were there for about a year. I was in a bad way and it took that long to recover. I remember trying to stay fit physically, by running, and spiritually, by writing a journal. But nothing seemed to shift the complete weariness that had come over me.

I had my 'flop friends' too – people Joyce and I could turn to, flop down on their sofa, and share with them all that was happening. They were able to listen and correct without any sense of accusation or of shock regarding my condition. I remember Jenny and Glen just turning up one time and taking the time to listen. David and Annabel did the same. Another time it was Steve and Mary. Another time, Barry and Kay. Mike and Jenny Jones kept a close eye on us. Mike as a pastor figure and a trained doctor was especially helpful; he loved me as a brother and kept me sane. And my best friend during this time was Joyce, of course. She was used to supporting me from behind, but had to take the lead, speak positively to me and pray for change. Despite her own problems with her health, she was, and remains, my best friend, greatest prayer partner and most faithful truth-affirming companion.

Benson Idahosa

A friend took us to a meeting in London, and because of our friend's connections, we found ourselves as VIPs on the front row. The speaker was Benson Idahosa, a man of God mightily used in revival in Nigeria.

During his preaching that night, he stopped. Looking at me, he came over and sat down next to me. The congregation weren't sure what was happening – and I certainly wasn't! Benson began to prophesy over me. He kept declaring, 'This is God's decree – it is over now.' As he said those words, something broke.

I had been trying to rest, to eat well, to exercise well. None of these things appeared to help my general condition. But as I received the decree from the Lord that night, God broke the power that had a hold of me. With the benefit of hindsight, I believe some kind of curse had been put on me, from one of the places we had been evangelising, and without my knowledge. God always wins though. And that night, the victory was won. I sensed something had happened. Within six weeks I was completely well, both physically and mentally.

An Indian pastor had helped me personally on the recent trip, in order to come to terms with being childless. Joyce and I had, together, to lay our desire for children at the foot of the cross. We were not able to have children, but God has given us so many 'adopted' children on our travels around the world. Even today, we have young people come and stay with us. We are blessed.

Local church

God had ministered to us with regard to being childless. And we were freed from whatever the curse was. But we felt we had not been protected spiritually. We had been flat out in ministry with YWAM and had neglected the need to be in the right local church and with the need to have prayer cover for all we were doing.

On reflection, a good link to a local church could have saved me a lot of pain. We all need a spiritual home. A place with friends who will be honest with us and pray for us. A pastor who cares. People who are not afraid to dive into difficult situations, speak the truth and help recovery. We had our friends, but it would have been better still to have had a local church supporting us as well.

In addition, a local church provides that extra prayer cover. Sometimes those out of the day-to-day pressures of a missionary organisation are better placed to pray, and to listen to the Holy Spirit directing their prayers. I know nowadays that my local church is absolutely essential to my protection when I travel on mission.

Lessons learned. And gratefulness to God that He will always come through for His children.

Chapter Fourteen
Don't Come!

As our year of recuperation came to an end, and we entered the decade of the 1990s, we had opened discussions with Pastor Ian Christensen, of New Life Christian Centre, Wembley. Ian, a good friend, had been praying for an evangelist to work alongside him for some time. We warmed to the idea of this particular church. It was part of the Assemblies of God denomination, and the people were clearly wanting all God had for them and for the church.

We began to make preparations to move. It was then the letter arrived.

The letter

The letter was from the (then) treasurer of the Wembley church and it basically said 'don't come'! The treasurer explained that they did not have the money for any salary and we would therefore not be welcome. It puzzled us. We had been praying for a while about this move and it had seemed right to us. We had even gone as far as sitting down with Pastor Ian to work out a role for Joyce as well. All these things had been settled and we were only a few weeks away from moving when the letter arrived. It sent us to our knees.

At the same time as the letter, we were approached by two friends regarding potential ministry moves. One friend wanted to move next door to us at our present address, buy both houses and start a ministry with us. Another friend offered us a house free of charge, with us working in their church as evangelists.

Both offers were considerably more generous that the offer from Wembley. But as the months rolled by, we had no peace at all regarding either of these kind approaches.

The house

Despite the letter, we started to look at new houses in the Wembley area. A fine-looking gentleman showed us around some properties. At the end of the tour, he took out a cigar and began to talk about finances.

'So, I wonder if I may ask you what you earn, please?'

'Well… We live by faith.'

'I'm sorry. What did you say?'

'We live by faith. We trust God for our income. There will be a small income from the church of about £12,000 a year. The rest will be provided. God never lets us down.'

The man's face began to turn red.

'You're wasting my time. You've just wasted the last two hours! You've wasted your petrol too. I suggest you turn around and drive back to Nuneaton and forget about today.'

With that, he blew cigar smoke in my face and walked away.

'Well,' I said to Joyce. 'We've just met someone with the ministry of discouragement!'

We began to pray: 'Lord, You heard that!'

I reminded God as to what the man had said. I pointed out to God how the man had treated us and asked God to answer. He did.

Within ten days we had been given £21,000. Both the friends who had given us other offers gave sacrificially to us as they saw

God in the Wembley move. In addition, many other friends gave £1,000 or £2,000 towards our housing, either as gifts or interest-free loans.

From the day we arrived at the church, the weekly offering went up on average by 17 per cent. The pastor was excited. The treasurer was silent!

Gangs

We had arrived. And we had arrived to a challenge. Wembley can be a difficult area to be in. There are big Muslim and Hindu communities. There's a large and mixed community from many nations, a lot of whom work in the entertainment industry in and around Wembley Stadium and Wembley Arena. There's a strong gay and transvestite community. And there are gangs. On more than one occasion, there were rival gang fights close to our church building.

Early on in our Wembley time, Joyce and I were in the car and stopped at a set of traffic lights. Suddenly two rival gangs started fighting in front of us. It looked ugly. Real damage was being done, both to gang members and to anything else in sight, such as the shops and bus shelter.

As they fought, they were getting nearer. I prayed.

'Lord, stop them! Satan, I rebuke you!'

Suddenly, one of the gang members shouted, 'Cops! The cops are here!' And with that, they ran off.

The funny thing was, there *were* no cops. Joyce and I looked around. There were no police in sight, nor did any arrive in the next few minutes we were there.

God had answered. He had protected us.

Bible school

The Children of God cult had been strong in the Wembley area. More than thirty of them ended up in our church one Sunday morning. They were messed up in so many ways, particularly sexually and mentally. Deep ministry was needed. Pastor Ian and I were not sure we had the ability to help them. But God was sure.

We witnessed God's mercy in action. How He ministered to children who had been abused sexually. How He changed the minds of those who had been mentally controlled. How He dealt with the anger of those who knew they had been duped by the cult. How He set people free from years of lies and abuse.

One of the keys was the new Bible school. Ian had been praying about it for a while before we established it. It was clear that those from the cult who came to the Bible school were the ones that got free first. No surprise, really – it was the power of the Word at work in people's lives.

It wasn't just the Bible school. Sundays were electric with the Holy Spirit. People were turning up every week, from all corners of society – businessmen, transvestites. News of the church got about. Healings were regular occurrences. It was a rare Sunday when someone didn't get saved and just as rare not to see a significant healing.

The church grew in just a few months from around sixty people to more than 300. Ian had a strong prayer ministry and I have no doubt that this undergirded the growth. He was serious about prayer and expected answers. Add to that my passion for evangelism, and it was an explosive mix. Our faith grew so much. As a leadership team we fully expected that God would save and heal at every single meeting.

I remember one particularly amazing healing. A lady asked us to pray for her back. She was completely stiff and couldn't bend. She had three metal rods in her back, inserted following an accident. We began to pray. As we did, we felt a heat in her back. She felt it too. A few minutes later, she was running up and down, stretching and touching her toes. God had completely healed her. She had no restrictions whatsoever in her movement.

Wrong attitudes

It wasn't all plain sailing. Ian was a close friend as well as being the pastor of the church. I found it hard to take his instructions and I was treating him too much as a friend; not enough as a leader. During the four years we were in the church, we worked well together but I have had to repent of my attitude towards him. Having a friend as your leader is not always a recipe for harmony.

While we were at Wembley, another friend became such a helper and mentor to us – Philip Mohabir. Philip was an apostle in his own right, having planted many churches and having helped to lead a number of church networks and groupings.[15] He took us under his wing.

I can remember the three questions he used to ask me every time we met:

- How are you treating your wife?
- How is your 'eye-gate'?
- How are your finances?

---

15. Ephesians 4:11-12 explains the role of an apostle is applicable for the church today. It can be defined as someone 'sent out' to build and establish churches.

They were perceptive questions and he got to speak into our lives at a deep level.

Indian hospital

Because of my own attitude to Ian, treating him too much as a friend, and not enough as a leader, I was regularly disagreeing with him. I felt the only solution was to move on. And I admit I was completely wrong. It was my own insecurity and immaturity. But I felt we needed to get away from Wembley. The possibility of a further mission to India came up, so we took it.

Our reasoning was wrong and we didn't really listen to the Lord as to whether we should go. We went to get out of a situation at home.

The mission itself, near the Nilgiri Hills in south India, was a great success. We preached to thousands and hundreds got saved. But on the last day of the mission, Joyce became ill.

She had been feeling some pain before the mission. The doctor hadn't been able to diagnose it, and eventually we decided to go on the mission anyway.

Thankfully, the church leader in India knew of a Christian hospital in Madurai. We met the senior surgeon, who was quickly able to diagnose the problem – gall stones. An operation was needed, and Joyce would then be in recovery for around six weeks. Thankfully the hospital waived the charges, realising we were living by faith.

As Joyce came out of the operating theatre, the surgeon had a worried look on his face.

'David, there were complications. The severity of the gall stones had begun to affect Joyce's other organs. If I hadn't operated today, she could well have been dead within a few days.'

I swallowed hard. Grateful to God on the one hand, and aware that this had been brought on partly by our own disobedience. My desire to run away from the situation at Wembley had meant we had travelled on a mission without the usual clarity as to whether we should go, and more importantly, without the prayer protection of a church back home. We would normally never travel on mission without certainty about the ministry and without prayer – especially to a country such as India where the devil parades himself through false gods in an open manner.

Nursing

Each day during Joyce's recovery, I would walk the half hour to the hospital and then back to my accommodation in the evening. I'd eat just once, at the hospital canteen, trying to preserve the little money we had.

It was while I was visiting that I noticed one of the nurses failing to take proper care with an intravenous drip. It's important that you check there are no air pockets, and she had failed to do so. Another nurse was injecting a patient without the appropriate preparation. With my training as a nurse, I was a little shocked, but not sure what to do. It turned out that most of the staff at the hospital had no formal qualifications, and with encouragement from the surgeon, I began to help train the staff.

The hospital also rescued children, especially girls, who were abandoned at birth due to being the 'wrong sex'. The financial pressure of a girl born into a poor family was due to the dowry system, still illegally in operation in many parts of India, where significant money has to be paid to the bridegroom's family upon marriage. Baby girls would be abandoned at birth as a result and the Christian hospital rescued these girls. The hospital staff would go looking for the babies. Many were found on rubbish tips; one in a black bag in a wheelie bin. Another was found in a public toilet. There were around sixty babies and children in the unit at that time, nearly all of them girls, and they were trophies of grace. I had the privilege of teaching the older ones and praying with them throughout Joyce's time in the hospital.

Even after six weeks, complications meant that Joyce needed further care. We were able to get flights to Malaysia, and Joyce's mother took control of the convalescence.

By God's grace, this is the only time we are aware of where we travelled in our 'own strength' instead of listening to the Holy Spirit first. As such, we were limiting the work and power of the Holy Spirit in our lives. When we travel in His strength and with His direction, God will keep us. When we step out of His will for our lives, we can inadvertently find ourselves exposed to the enemy. We ran away from the church in Wembley when we should have stayed and seen it through. Our naivety nearly took Joyce's life. Lesson learned again.

Chapter Fifteen
'You Should Have Been Here Years Ago'

I listened nervously to the phone ringing.

'Hello, Colin Urquhart here.'

'Colin, hi, it's David. Er... I don't quite know how to put this. Joyce and I have been praying. We know our time in Wembley is coming to an end, and the more we pray, the more Kingdom Faith keeps coming to our minds. We so appreciated being some of your first students, but... well.... we were wondering whether there was any possibility of working with you again?'

I had stumbled through the words, partly embarrassed, partly not sure what to say. I didn't want to be presumptuous. I didn't want to be rejected, either!

I needn't have worried.

'David, you should have been here years ago!'

We'd known Colin for many years, of course. He was a regular visitor to St Mark's and when he had set up Kingdom Faith Ministries, we had been some of his first students. Since then, we had kept in touch and it was exciting to see how the college at Roffey Place near Horsham had grown under Colin and Bob Gordon's tutelage.

An interview with Dan Chesney followed. Dan has a Masters in Clinical Psychology, so quite a bit of psychoanalysis was thrown in. It was strange for me, but seemingly I passed the interview. I was to be appointed as Director of Missions and as evangelist to the ministry.

It was a high-powered appointment in comparison to what I had been used to. A church had grown from Kingdom Faith Ministries and at the time it was still meeting at Roffey Place (later it would get its own building in Horsham). The church meetings were amazing – powerful encounters with the Holy Spirit.

Street preaching

One of my initiatives was to take the students out each Friday onto the streets of Horsham; often as many as twenty or thirty students at a time. This became a regular event. Joyce formed a drama group to help with the presentations on the street.

These times were dynamic. Lots of noise and colour. A clear preaching of the gospel, and many finding a faith in Christ right there on the streets as we prayed with them.

One of our students at the time, Simon Breaker (now a prayer and prophetic minister at Holy Trinity Church, Leicester) had a crazy idea. We ended up putting Simon in a real coffin and carrying it to the town centre, with all of us dressed in black. As we laid the coffin down, Simon broke out, jumped to his feet and preached the resurrection power of Christ!

On a visit to Crawley, Joyce and I found twenty-five Muslims witnessing to their faith in the shopping centre. I began to talk to them. I could tell it was having an impact on the two guys I was specifically talking to. After a while, the leader of the group was called over. He was much more aggressive: 'You Christians! You come to your faith decisions without one ounce of intelligence!'

It made me cross to hear him speaking like that. I replied, 'You don't know me and you don't know my faith journey. You are full of pride and on your way to hell. You need to repent and accept Jesus.'

I put my hand on his head and rebuked the devil. The power of God hit the man – we could see him physically shaken by it as he jumped back in surprise.

He announced, 'This guy is crazy! Come on, pack up, we're leaving.'

I'm not sure my approach was the right one. In fact, I am sure it wasn't. But God even used my anger to bring the power of the Holy Spirit into the situation. I pray the power encounter shook the man enough for him to genuinely seek Jesus Christ.

The care homes

Joyce and I got to know a lady who ran five care homes for older people and for those with learning difficulties. She approached me and asked whether as a church we would be willing to partner with her and spend time with the residents, taking them out and talking to them. Tragically, some of the residents had no visitors, and if it were not for the staff, they would receive no birthday cards or presents.

'But,' said the lady, 'none of that Jesus stuff!'

I assured her that our faith would show itself anyway, in the way we worked with our new friends. And sure enough, that's what happened. We were welcomed by the residents and spent many hours with them. A good number found a faith simply by the way we witnessed through our work with them.

There was a different kind of care happening as well. I helped train up a good number of church people in how to welcome visitors on Sunday and care for them after the meeting. This included taking those from their row in the meeting for coffee afterwards and leading them to Christ if they were not already Christians. Through this ministry, we were seeing as many as thirty people a month coming to a living faith in Christ.

Joyce and I were always looking for ways to encourage the church in evangelism. Part of my gifting as an evangelist must always be to encourage and train others, not just to do the stuff myself. We were able to identify 'hotspots' around the church home groups where people were being attracted to the groups and then finding faith. We then spent time with the leaders of those home groups, to help them do even better in reaching their friends and neighbours.

Healing

Healing has always been part of Colin Urquhart's ministry. I began to extend the healing ministry further. When people without a Christian faith get healed, they tend to get saved too. The two go hand in hand. I was keen to see what Jesus would do.

One outreach resulted in a fifty-year-old man being healed in his left ear. He then came to a special healing meeting we were running and found a faith in Christ. On his way back to his seat, near the end of the meeting, he stopped at my chair. Leaning over, he said, 'Fix the other one, please!'

I loved his faith and prayed for his other ear to be healed. It was. As a result, he sent the hearing aids back to his doctor, saying he no longer needed them. Unsurprisingly, the doctor called him in for an appointment. At the end of the session, the doctor turned to him and said, pointing to the hearing aids, 'You don't need these any more!'

Kingdom Faith has regularly held a Faith Camp each year at the Peterborough Showground. Over my time with Kingdom Faith, I had the privilege of speaking there on a number of occasions. Each time, I would ensure the gospel was preached, with healing offered. It's amazing how at a Bible camp, there are so many that don't have a living faith. Joyce and I were able to pray with many over the years to find a genuine faith in Christ.

While at the Faith Camp, we would take teams into Peterborough and arrange for special healing meetings. It was there that we met Peter. Peter was giving out Christian tracts in the main square from his motorised wheelchair. At our evening healing meeting, I called him to the front and we began to pray for his healing. I invited him to get out of his wheelchair and walk. He did.

At that same time in a church meeting in Bradford, his wife, who was also wheelchair-bound, was prayed for. She also got out of her wheelchair and walked.

Some months later, Peter called on me at Kingdom Faith at Roffey Place. He and his wife were still walking. God had completely healed them both.

Toronto

By the middle of 1994, a number of the leaders had either been over to the Toronto Airport Vineyard Church or to Rodney Howard-Browne meetings in the UK. God was moving in an unusual and refreshing way during this time, sparked originally by meetings at Toronto which quickly spread to churches around the world. There is no doubt that we benefited back at Roffey Place from the meetings the leaders attended. Dan Chesney was particularly affected by the moving of the Holy Spirit. At one staff gathering, he got up to preach but promptly fell under the power of the Spirit after just a few words.

On Sundays it was common for most of the congregation to be on the floor by the end of the time together, sensing a powerful anointing of the Holy Spirit. Those who came in for the second service would regularly need to step over the bodies still on the floor.

All generations were appreciating this refreshing of the Holy Spirit. Children and teenagers wanted to be in the main meetings rather than have their own. At the end of the Sunday meetings, some in the congregation were so 'drunk' in the Spirit, they were unable to walk for some hours afterwards. We even saw some returning to their cars in the car park, but on their hands and knees, still affected by the Holy Spirit. I trust they weren't driving!

Meetings would be full of laughter. But at the same time, we were meeting with God in a deep and extraordinary way. Many deep needs and hurts were met by God and ministered to through the Spirit, often as someone was simply on the floor under the Holy Spirit's anointing. They would eventually get up, knowing God had met them in a life-changing way, with issues that had not been dealt with for years suddenly sorted out as they rested on the carpet.

'Jesus, don't go!'

Richard Heard, a pastor from Houston, Texas, came to speak at one of our larger gatherings. God had recently met his congregation in an unusual way. As Richard was about to introduce his visiting speaker, Tommy Tenney, he first read a Bible passage, calling on God to move in power. As he finished reading, Richard looked up and said: 'The word of the Lord to us is to stop seeking His benefits and seek Him. We are not to seek His hand any longer, but seek His face.'

At that moment, there was a sound like a thunderclap. Richard was picked up by the Spirit and thrown backwards. The thick Perspex pulpit his Bible was resting on was split in two by the power of God.

Needless to say, this got the attention of the congregation. So dynamic was this visible manifestation that many felt an awesome fear of God. Some saw angels. Others spontaneously experienced miraculous healings and demonstrations of the Spirit. For almost three months, unpredictable services focused on repentance and seeking God's face. It left a perpetual anointing on his congregation.

As Richard shared his story to the 1,000 or so gathered at Kingdom Faith, every one of us seemed to be stirred by the Spirit. That night Joyce and I ran to the front at the end of the meeting, desperate to meet God in the way Richard had so eloquently explained. As I knelt at the front, I saw Jesus. He was standing in front of me. Then He began to turn and make His way to the door at that back. At this point I shouted out at the top of my voice: 'Jesus, don't go!'

Others were crying and shouting too. Many were saying the same thing: 'Jesus, don't go!'

At that point I saw Him turn again. He looked at me and I felt Him tell me that He would stay – but that it would mean some changes. I felt myself undone. I saw all of my sin. And I saw Jesus, lovingly looking at me, as if to say I was forgiven and He would be with me.

I don't recall much of the hour or so after that except, at the end of the evening, I looked down onto the wooden floor and saw a pool of water in front of me, and realised they were my tears.

In Germany, at around that time, we led a meeting of about 1,000 people. I had felt that God was going to reveal to me something of a prelude to revival in that meeting; and He did. The meeting seemed to go on for just a few minutes, but when we looked at our watches, it had been going on for four hours. Again there was a similar Holy Spirit anointing in that meeting. At the back of the meeting, about an hour in, I noticed a number of young people arrive. They were dressed in black with heavy black make-up and declared themselves as 'goths'. They appeared to want to break up the meeting. But no sooner were they through the door than they too were falling to the floor. Many received deliverance ministry that night and all were saved.

After about seven months of the Spirit moving in this way in Kingdom Faith, Colin felt to bring it to an end. He believed we had received and it was time to move on to what God had for us next. What we witnessed with Colin was an increase in his apostolic anointing. Colin felt he had rejected the original call of God to serve as an apostle, but with the quickening of the Holy Spirit during this time, he received a confirmation of his calling. The months that followed were a time of growth and Colin moved in an increased anointing. God was with us. We all had an increased understanding of God's grace and how much He loved us.

The books

It was during our time with Kingdom Faith that I felt I heard God telling me to put down in writing something of what I had been learning. It was a strange one for me. Because of my background, I wasn't sure I would be the most natural of writers, but the nagging of the Holy Spirit was pretty incessant, so I set to work.

The first book was from my heart as an evangelist. It's a practical handbook for effective evangelism and is entitled *Keys to the Harvest*. Colin was kind enough to provide a Foreword, and he also encouraged the publishers, Hodder & Stoughton, to go for it. The second, two years later in 1999, just as we were leaving Kingdom Faith, was called *Angels & Demons*. Joyce and I have carried out a lot of ministry in the area of deliverance, but there seemed to be quite a gap in the church's understanding as to what the Bible says about our authority over demons and also about the angels that live around us. Zondervan published this one, and again, Colin was kind enough to promote it and offer a Foreword.

Years later, I again felt the prompting of the Holy Spirit for one more book. And that's what you have in your hands today.

Chapter Sixteen
East Africa

Joyce and I found that the missions we went on during the time that God was blessing the UK with the Holy Spirit outpouring were different kinds of missions. It seems we took that particular blessing with us. During our Kingdom Faith missions in Kenya and Uganda, we found that as we prayed and ministered, people would immediately fall under the power of the Spirit. There would be much laughter and a good deal of healing, just as at home – despite the fact that before our visit, there had been no such move of the Spirit. We sat in a pastor's home in Kenya, and just as we began to share about what God had been doing at Roffey Place, both the pastor and his wife fell to the floor under the power of the Holy Spirit.

Our friends Mike and Coral Parsons were working in Uganda. They had chosen to live in an area that in the past had suffered the most terrible atrocities under the dictatorship of the former president Idi Amin, and from other tribal wars. The Luweero District they worked in had seen rebel groups fighting right through what became known as the 'Bush Wars' of the 1980s. As a result, the area was called locally the 'Killing Fields'. Since that time, many children had been orphaned by the AIDS epidemic. It was such a needy area, and neglected by other missions.

What started from a small UK-based trust with very little money grew rapidly as God blessed them. Soon they had their own coffee plantation to help bring in more funds. They developed a family complex, an orphanage housing sixty children and a school. Joyce and I took teams out from Kingdom Faith to help them.

I would often find myself in tears as my team joined the children in worship. We met Mercy there. Now into her teenage years, as a child she had seen all her family murdered in one of the tribal wars. She had also been shot, but only in the leg. She came around to find that she was the only one of her family still alive. But there she was with a full and open heart to God, praising Him for all He had given. It was humbling to see. Tears flowed. What I witnessed in the orphanage has left its mark on me and I count it as one of the highlights of my Christian life to have seen these children, who have lost so much, completely set free from their past as Jesus has healed them internally and externally.

In one meeting, after showing the *Jesus* film, we announced that we had a God of miracles and God could heal anyone. A young boy was brought to the front. He had learning difficulties and was both deaf and dumb. As we prayed for him, I felt a particular anointing of God's Spirit hit the boy. He immediately began to speak for the first time in his life, and in fluent English! His mental abilities had also been fully restored. It's fair to say the miracle attracted a lot of attention. There were many more healed. More importantly, as we continued to show the *Jesus* film, there were many hundreds who found a saving faith in Christ.

Alcohol

During that same visit to Uganda, I was up early one morning as the postman arrived. I could smell alcohol on his breath. Immediately the Holy Spirit gave me a picture of him under a big tree with a lot of other men, all of them drinking. I shared the picture with the postman and he began to cry. Coming into the house, we gathered around him and began to pray for him, especially that he be released from his alcohol addiction. As I started to cast out the demon of alcohol from him, suddenly the whole house began to reek of alcohol. This lasted a minute or so, but as the demon went, so the smell cleared. The man was completely sober with no remaining smell of alcohol on his breath. Better still, that Sunday, he was in the church meeting with his family, testifying to what God had done and that he had remained completely free from alcohol.

Near the end of our stay with Mike and Coral, we set up a banquet, and invited all the chieftains, leaders and dignitaries from the Luweero District. More than 100 came. I preached at the end of the meal for over an hour and a good number of them gave their lives to Christ.

Joyce and I have regularly visited Uganda and Kenya and have taken teams from whatever church we have been in at the time. The teams come back changed, of course. We give, but the local Christians give back to us and I have witnessed many British Christians changed forever by such trips, with a better world view and greater understanding of God's kingdom at work today.

Monsoons

Regular visits to Kenya have seen many people giving their lives to Christ. Not in the same numbers that I had been used to, though, in other African countries. It troubled me at first, but I noticed that the 'discipleship rate' was much higher. In other words, if only ten men were saved in a meeting, all ten would go on with Christ and join a local church, putting an end to womanising, drinking and smoking. Part of the reason is due to earlier revivals which have left their mark on the nation of Kenya. People know what it means to follow Christ, so when they do accept Christ, it means more to them than may be the case in a country with no revival history.

One of the ways we got people's attention – and it happened in Kenya more than other nations – was by stopping the monsoon rains. We would often be about to go out onto the streets to witness to locals when the heavens would open. We became expectant that God would answer our prayers for the rain to immediately stop. God answered this prayer so often. At one time, in a market square, with everyone watching, we called out to God as the rains started. No sooner had we shouted out our prayer than the rain petered out to nothing.

With the street preaching finished, we moved on, in the evenings, to crusades in the various Kenyan towns and villages. We would set up a stage with sound equipment. Word got around and 5,000 or more people would arrive for most of those events.

I would pray and ask God for words of knowledge, which would then raise faith levels. At the start of one meeting, I announced that there was a deaf and dumb girl in the congregation and please could the parents bring her to the front. Immediately, a woman came to the front, holding the hand of a little girl of four or five years old. The girl came onto the stage with her mother and we prayed. Instantly her hearing was restored and immediately she began to speak a few words in her local language. The first word she said was 'Mummy'. I had a speech therapist on the team who was able to verify what had happened and teach the girl how to speak further.

What we didn't know was that this miracle quickly became known in all the villages. There was a deaf and dumb boy living wild in the bush who was told the story through a friend. He walked for two solid days to get to the meeting. When he arrived, the meeting was already in full flow and I was speaking. He came straight to the front, got my attention and asked for prayer. He didn't care that there was a meeting going on – he had walked for two days and wanted healing. What faith!

I prayed for him, and he was instantly healed, right there, half way through my preaching.

The secret weapon

On one of our Kenyan missions, my mother-in-law came along. She was seventy years old at the time. I was concerned she would be a bit old for some of the rural areas we were visiting, but felt the prompting of the Holy Spirit to invite her.

We got to know the owner of the hotel chain we were using on the trip. She was a lovely lady, but was struggling with her husband, who was a known womaniser and often came home drunk. We had the opportunity one evening to talk with him. It seemed to me that whatever Joyce and I said, he simply tuned us out and showed no interest. But when my mother-in-law began to share her faith, he listened. This is because of the context. In Kenya, older people are revered within the culture, so when my mother-in-law spoke, he listened. By the end of the evening, he had asked Jesus to change his life. We could see a significant change straight away. He was reputedly one of the richest people in Kenya and I was grateful that God was interested in the rich as well as the poor.

We got a phone call from his wife a little while later.

'What did you do? My husband is completely different! He is coming to church with me. He has stopped drinking and he has avoided all contact with other women. How did that happen? What did you say?'

'Well,' I said. 'I used my secret weapon – my mother-in-law!'

I love the way God uses all sorts of circumstances. At an animal market, I prayed for a sickly calf. It was immediately healed, which got the interest of the owners! In fact, God has used me a few times in this way. On a holiday in Florida, I once asked God to raise a horse from the dead. I persisted in prayer for about twenty minutes. Suddenly it began to breathe again. It gets people's attention.

Television

Since our early missions into Kenya with Kingdom Faith, friendships have grown and opportunities have increased. One of those opportunities was to get involved with a weekly television broadcast.

In 2002, GOD TV set up a new television mast in Eldorat, Kenya. They started to transmit quite a number of the programmes broadcast in the UK. Their local partner, Sayare TV, wanted programmes that were more appropriate to Kenya and the adjoining nations. Having preached in one of the churches in Eldorat, I was known to the local owner and as a result began a weekly half-hourly television programme. I aimed the programme at locals as much as possible with, of course, clear gospel content. Because I was only travelling to Kenya every six months or so, I would record six months of programmes in one go. This was exhausting – both physically in terms of keeping going, and spiritually in terms of seeking God for content and ensuring the content was varied.

GOD TV dropped out of the partnership and I ended up, along with others, partnering with the local Christian TV company. The programme has an estimated reach to 31 million people. The owner also has a radio station and I have broadcast for them as well. The most notable radio broadcast I recall was when the people in the studio started to get healed as some local children prayed for the Holy Spirit to come in healing, all live on-air.

I spoke on one occasion regarding what I felt God was telling me about the nation of Kenya. I felt that God was bringing a warning regarding impending political trouble. I quoted the famous passage from 2 Chronicles in the Old Testament: 'if My people who are called by My name will humble themselves, and pray and seek My face, and turn from their wicked ways, then I will hear from heaven, and will forgive their sin and heal their land.'[16] I called for a national day of prayer in order to avoid potential bloodshed.

Unbeknown to me, one of those watching the broadcast was high up in the Kenyan government and he brought the broadcast to the attention of the vice president. The vice president alerted

16. 2 Chronicles 7:14, NKJV.

the president to the story, and a national day of prayer was called as a result. The day was taken seriously by the people and we witnessed many even kneeling in the streets on that day, praying for their nation.

A few months later, trouble came. Two politicians both claimed victory in disputed local elections in a number of parts of the country. Bloodshed followed, but remarkably, unlike earlier uprisings, this one didn't get off the ground. It stopped within a few days and there was no escalation – something that had been seen regularly in earlier political disputes. I'm grateful to God for answering the prayers; and to the Kenyan government for listening to the warnings and calling for the day of prayer.

The Turkanas

Over the years, we have worked particularly among the desert-living Turkana tribes of north-west Kenya. This involves four-wheel-drive off-roading to get there, and then living in tents when we do. And it can be hot there! I remember it getting as high as 46 degrees Celsius. It was hard to breathe, let alone preach. By God's grace, through the many team visits, we have seen more than 600 of these wonderful tribal people saved, and at least two churches planted.

We have worked with the tribe to provide water. I have been able to team up with businessmen and see a number of bore holes successfully dug in order to provide water in the villages. We are starting to build schools and have built a watchman's house near the main well.

God has moved miraculously among the tribe too. I wonder

whether part of the reason for this is simply His kindness and grace to a people that have no access to doctors or medicines. On one visit in 2016, we saw those who couldn't walk healed, we witnessed the deaf hear, we heard the dumb speak – and twenty-seven people healed of blindness. Twenty-seven! What a God of miracles we serve.

I was so stirred by the twenty-seven miracles of people receiving their sight. The very next day, walking out into the local village, I saw a young man leading his mother. She was blind, deaf and dumb. I asked if I could pray for her blindness to go. The young man agreed. I prayed for nearly forty-five minutes without any noticeable change. Then she began to speak. God had healed her of deafness and dumbness, while I was praying for her eyes! I think God really does have a sense of humour! I don't know if she saw at a later time – that is always possible when we pray; all miracles are not immediate. I remember the look on the young man's face as they walked away; his mother could hear and speak and he was overjoyed. I pray the rest of the miracle followed.

Chapter Seventeen
A Change of Clothes

Joyce had been waiting a long time. God had given a word to her before we met that she would marry a pastor. Instead, in her own words, she had married a 'raving evangelist'. But God was true to His word.

During our five years with Kingdom Faith, Joyce and I had travelled on many occasions to preach at various churches in the UK. One of those had been Ashford Christian Fellowship (ACF) in Kent. Our good friend from our nursing days, Joyce G, and her husband had moved there and we had the privilege of speaking at the church a number of times.

The church had been started around 1981 by its founders Syd and Liz Doyle. They had been in place all the way through until 1999, although for the final two years, they were in the States a lot. They had moved to Michigan in order to pick up on some additional studies, and had then felt to stay there. Liz was from the States originally, so for her, it was going home.

We knew them quite well, but despite that, it was a surprise to be asked by them to consider taking on ACF. I joke that at that point, I made a mistake. Instead of saying 'No, I'm an evangelist,' I agreed to pray about it.

As I prayed, God did a remarkable thing in me. He caused me to want to be a pastor. It was as if a new 'mantle' had been thrown over my shoulders. In the Bible, mantles or cloaks are used at moments of significant change. For example, Elijah throws his cloak over Elisha and this indicates that the call of God on Elijah is passing to Elisha.[17]

In my spirit, I felt God was throwing a new cloak or mantle over me – that of a pastor. It was as if God was giving me a change of clothes.

I shared the story with Joyce.

'I know.'

'What do you mean, you know? I haven't told you before!'

'No. I know you are going to be a pastor.'

'How?'

'Because God told me.'

When?'

'Before I met you.'

And that was it. God's word was being fulfilled all these years later. Like Mary, Joyce had stored these thoughts away[18] and now the word was being fulfilled.

They didn't laugh at my jokes!

Joyce and I went to Ashford for the weekend and on the Sunday I preached. It was not a good morning. I found the congregation unresponsive, and they didn't even laugh at my jokes. I found that a little disturbing and wondered whether I had misheard the call of the Lord for us. But looking back, I think they were all a bit unsure themselves. With Syd and Liz having been there since the beginning, new leadership was a big change for them.

---

17. See 1 Kings 19:19.
18. See Luke 2:19.

It wasn't long before we were planning our move – though that was also tested.

Simon Breaker, mentioned earlier, a man with a prophetic ministry in Leicester and one of our former students at Kingdom Faith, contacted us.

'Dave, I think this move will be challenged. You need to know that getting a house won't be easy. But also know that this is the call of God for you.'

I felt we could have done without a word like that, but of course, it was immensely helpful in holding on when the house move didn't come through.

Maybe it was partly my own fault. Having seen a house, I would insist on praying first before making an offer. By the time I contacted the estate agents, the house had gone. This happened on a number of occasions. Our belongings were stacked at the back of the church building for quite a while, but eventually the house came through.

And despite them not laughing at the jokes, I quickly felt part of this family. In fact, I felt different altogether. I had a pastor's heart for them. I wanted to be with them. All my longings to travel the world seemed to disappear. I wanted to be home. I wanted those in ACF to flourish and grow in God. God really had thrown a different cloak over my shoulders.

Classic errors

I didn't make it easy for the congregation, though. I was by this time in my fifties and this was my first real pastoral role. I made all the classic mistakes. At first, I found it hard to make decisions

– we needed blinds on the windows and it was almost a shock to me to find that I could make those decisions and get on with it.

On the other hand, I pushed too hard with some issues. A movement was finding its legs in the UK called G12. It was a principle of discipleship which originated in Colombia with Pastor César Castellanos. The idea was that each leader would be in a group of twelve for discipleship and we each would then choose a group of twelve. But the outworking of this is fraught with difficulties. Once you 'choose' your twelve, you aren't supposed to change. What about those that feel left out? What about the rigidity of always meeting as twelve? What about the different culture in the UK?

I was determined we were going to be a G12 church and basically said as much to the people, inferring that if they didn't like it, they should leave and find another church. Many of them did just that.

G12 may work for some, but it didn't for us. Around 100 people left the church over this time. Part of that was to do with my own unbending attitude to the process, and maybe partly to do with the unhelpfulness of this particular model in a UK church climate. There's a lot that is good about G12, not least the visionary aspect, and we have kept that as much as we can. But we have accepted that the demands of the restrictive G12 approach didn't work for us.

Releasing the men

It was clear that the church was stronger among the women than it was with the men. I wanted to change this, so started a men's prayer meeting every Sunday morning at 5am. Despite the day and the hour, around twenty to thirty men attended most Sundays. This really was a breakthrough.

It was hard, but so worth it. Getting up at 4am required diligence. I felt terrible at that time in the morning. But the more we pushed through as men together, the more successful we were in getting to the meeting; and successful in terms of answered prayer.

In addition, Joyce and I felt God saying that the women should stop some of their ministry for a time – this they did with good grace. I even put the men on the front row of the church, asking them to pray for me while I preached. The effect was immediate. A combination of the women stepping back, the men moving forward in prayer and the visibility of the men in the Sunday meeting resulted in a number of key men finding their ministries and the church moving forward on a number of fronts. It wasn't long before we were able to re-release the ladies in ministry and the church came into a time of anointing because everyone was involved.

God blessed us in many ways; me included. I found myself as chaplain of the British Legion, chair of the Ashford Pastors Fellowship and on a number of church executive groups. Thinking back to where I had come from, there is no other way of saying it than God is a God of the miraculous!

An international church

The Indian prophet looked up and pointed to Joyce and me. We were in a meeting where people didn't know us, and the man with the microphone certainly didn't know us.

'Sir and madam. Yes, you! God is changing your church. You are going to have an international church. God will bring in the nations.'

Joyce and I looked at each other and smiled. Because of our own background with missions, we longed for our church to be more representative of different nations, but at the time it was very white and very English.

Within months of this prophetic word, people began to join us from other nations. We decided that each time someone joined us from a different part of the world we would put up the flag of that nation in the church building. Eighteen months after the prophetic word, we counted forty-six different flags. This was God's doing.

The pattern of nations in the church is reflected in international missions as well. We still regularly visit the Philippines. We've visited France and Hong Kong. Recently we sent teams to Zimbabwe, Kenya, Mexico and South Africa. Add to that three UK missions this year – we're an active church. On most of our mission trips we see the Holy Spirit move in power during the worship. It is quite something to see more than 5,000 people in the Philippines come under the Spirit collectively, falling to the floor together, unable to move due to the particular presence of God in the meeting.

On one occasion, I took ten men with me to Guyana, to a church in a poor area – an area with a high crime rate and a drugs problem. On that mission, we built a church and community building. That was followed up with teaching and preaching trips. Our influence there, and the buildings we put up, improved the whole area. The drugs influence lessened, the value of the properties increased, and others wanted to build on the same street because of the perception that it was an improving area.

Zimbabwe

We've worked with churches in Zimbabwe since we started at ACF. One of our leaders, Mary, is from Zimbabwe. She went out to minister in the Kwekwe and Shabani areas. While there, the churches asked her about her home church. Mary was astonished to find that they all knew me – my Kenya TV programmes had reached them.

This was the start of a long relationship. I go out there most years, and if I can't go, I send a team. We have prayed for and prophesied over those regions for years. We have seen high unemployment reduce to one of the lowest in Zimbabwe. We have seen new mines open and new roads built. We have seen the churches grow and prosper as God does His work. We have spent nights in prayer for the region and have prayed over many of the politicians in person. We work with around fifty pastors. Five churches have been planted and many students sponsored. We support a children's home. Hundreds have been saved in crusades, and many released from demons. There have been many miracles. We have permission to pray in the hospitals and there are many miracles there too. The deaf and mute are healed, the blind see.

When we first went there, we spoke of restoration and regeneration. God has done it. The area has been transformed through prayer and faithful witness.

The effect on our local church of sending people to the nations has been profound. Those on mission have grown in faith; they have come back different, and have been able to contribute locally at an increased faith level. One young man went on mission even though he was allergic to mosquito bites. His whole body would swell up if he was bitten. But he went because he felt God telling him to. He was the only member of the team not to get bitten. Today he leads a church in another part of the UK and takes his own church teams out. A young couple saw almost everyone they prayed for in Zimbabwe healed. They brought that same healing ministry back to the UK and God is using them mightily here. To me, these steps of faith with people on mission are as great as the actual healing miracles we see in the meetings while we are out there, because of the impact it has back home.

Chapter Eighteen
Betrayal

God was answering prayers. The men had stepped up. The church was growing. People from many nations were added. I was enjoying this new role as a pastor.

It was during this time that I appointed two elders: Azariah and Casper. They were a great help to me. I loved their faith levels. They had come to us through our contacts in Africa and were clearly good leaders. I asked Casper to take on the treasurer role in the church.

I was naïve. I didn't appreciate that working out relationships as leaders together needs time and energy. I didn't fully appreciate the different mindset that many African leaders have regarding church. By the time I realised, it was too late.

The ladies' ministry

'I'm sorry, pastor, I can't make tonight's meeting. I'm at the ladies meeting.'

'Oh, is that a cross-church meeting? I'm sorry, I didn't know about it.'

'No,' said the woman. 'It's the one Magenta has arranged.'

Magenta was Casper's wife. She was a fiery woman and God had used her a lot in Africa in difficult situations before they came to the UK. We had given Casper and Magenta quite a high profile within the church. They were greatly appreciated for their leadership. But here, it seemed, was Magenta holding her own meeting on the same night as a church meeting, without our knowledge. It had been going on for months. By the time Joyce and I heard about it, it was too late. Casper and Magenta were well on their way to forming their own church. They had even set up a trust and some of the ladies at Magenta's meeting had started to give regularly to the trust rather than to the church. I felt betrayed. This was my fellow elder. My treasurer and his wife. Setting up a new church under our noses.

The prophetess Sharon Stone happened to be visiting at the time, and she agreed to meet with me and Joyce, Casper and Magenta. Sharon explained that if they wanted to start their own church, that was not a problem, but that it would be best to start one at least fifty miles away, in order to prove the calling and not take any of our own people.

They started their church in the next street.

Broken

Every emotion imaginable was at work in me at the time. I felt like I was having a breakdown. I was stressed, not sleeping.

I would get up in the middle of the night and pace the floor downstairs, thinking about what had happened and rehearsing my reply in the imaginary meeting I was having with Casper and Magenta. I became depressed. I wasn't doing the day job very well at all, and was constantly asking God whether I could leave the role as a pastor and return to being a straightforward evangelist.

My anger was on show to any that asked about the situation. I needed help but didn't know where to turn. I felt a broken man.

'Azariah, how has this happened?' I asked. 'Casper is your

friend. You are both from the same country in Africa. Am I missing something? Why are he and Magenta doing this?'

My ever-faithful friend Azariah would just smile and pray for me. He went through his own challenges in this as well. Casper connected up with an apostolic person in Africa who asked Azariah why he wasn't working with Casper. Azariah's reply was so appreciated: 'Do you want me to follow my friend, or do you want me to follow God?'

Casper was working his way through the congregation, inviting them to join him. Because he had been my treasurer, he knew the good tithers – those that regularly paid into the church – and he started by approaching them. He took a big file with him. In it, he had papers that purported to show what I was doing wrong and why God would not bless our church. I could see it happening in front of me. Many people were telling me what was happening. But I was helpless to do anything about it. Later I heard that there had even been 'spies in the camp';[19] people who had said they were with us, but were reporting back to Casper and Magenta. In the end, around twenty people left the church.

Added to that, it was as if the devil was targeting our church. Joyce and I were dealing with three other significant pastoral issues. I complained to God about that too. His reply was humorous: 'But you asked Me to clean up the church. That's what I'm doing!'

It's not all grace and glory

I'm aware that in these pages, there are many stories of miracles. On occasion in our lives, we have seen miracles and healing on

---

19. See Joshua 2.

a daily basis. We have felt close to God and have been blessed to serve. But it's not all grace and glory.

There are times as a leader when it gets pretty dark. When God seems to be a million miles away. When you stare at your Bible and all you see is words.

There have been a number of such occasions in my life and the betrayal was the worst of them. On a very human level, it's horrible to be betrayed, especially by people you loved and honoured. People you worked with in leadership. People you thought you knew and whom you trusted.

I felt such a fool. To have let this happen right in front of me and not to have seen it, simply hurt. Part of it was pride on my part, of course. I didn't want others to see my fallibility. And I hope that part was also a godly anger for what happened.

So, when you read these pages and bless God for His goodness, remember to stay close to Him. Remember that His ways are not ours;[20] that He will have His way and we can trust Him in that. He is the same yesterday, today and forever.[21] He is the same when we are rejoicing in miracles before our eyes and the same when we feel let down and abandoned.

The dream

I was a mess. But God has a habit of working with those of us who are in a mess, and bringing out the best.

For me, it started with a dream.

---

20. See Isaiah 55:8.
21. See Hebrews 13:8.

At the time, we had a Nigerian pastor staying with us, Pastor Christie. She was a little lady, with a big passion for God. As we told her our story, a frown appeared on her face. At the end of our sharing with her, with our emotions so obviously on show, she stood up. Pointing her bony finger right at me, she said: 'This has to stop. The Lord says to you it's time to move on from this!' I felt the rebuke. And I felt it was from the Lord. In my turmoil, I had taken hold of the hurt and bitterness and twisted it around in such a way that it had a hold of me. I had been nursing my hurt. I was paralysed; unable to hear God's voice properly and on the verge of a breakdown.

But that moment from Pastor Christie released me. And that night God spoke.

In a dream, I heard God's voice speaking to me through Scripture: '"Rejoice in the Lord always: and again I say, Rejoice" … "all things work together for good to them that love God" … David, are you practising those scriptures?'[22]

In the dream, I started to cry and to repent. I knew very well that I hadn't been practising those scriptures. I hadn't been living those scriptures.

Then I saw it happen. In the dream, as I was crying and repenting, I saw a demon leave me and I knew what it was – it was a demon of grief.

As I woke, I felt no different. But I started to speak out the scriptures from the dream. At first it was just a mechanical rote, but as I continued to do it, I felt a freshness come over me. I felt the Holy Spirit lifting my head and giving me hope.

---

22. Philippians 4:4; Romans 8:28, KJV.

'Today God is going to heal you'

Dan Chesney, our fellow leader from our time with Kingdom Faith, was the visiting speaker that next Sunday. He was aware of what had happened, but had none of the detail.

As he got up to preach, he stopped. Looking around the congregation, he lifted his hand and began to point at each of us.

'Today God is going to heal you. Today it's over.'

As Dan said the words, there was a sense of God the Holy Spirit invading the place. As suddenly as the words had been spoken, it was over. There and then at the start of Dan's preaching, God lifted the heartache. Every one of us was spiritually healed at that moment. As we compared notes afterwards, it was as if God had wiped our minds clean of all that had troubled us about the church split. The ugliness of it was gone. There was no more hurt; no more bitterness. It was all gone.

As a postscript to what happened, a year or two later, Casper and Magenta's boy became ill with meningitis. We prayed as a church and I had a picture of him dying but coming back to life. Later, we learned that this was what had happened. He had been brought back to life by way of cardiopulmonary resuscitation (CPR).

A week or two later, Casper came to the door.

'David, I know you were praying as a church. I have come to say thank you.'

We are still working out the healing of our relationship, but that was a good start.

Lessons

For me, there were again lessons to be learned. How I needed to lean on God, give Him my feelings, allow His Spirit to work in me and not to hold onto the grudges and hurts that are inevitably offered by the devil for me to consume. I felt I was a hopeless pastor and it is only in recent years that I have learned that what I went through is common to many churches. Lord, forgive us.

As I look back today, I believe I grew in my walk with God faster through this event than at any other time in my life. This is priceless. Money can't buy it. Teaching and theology can't impart it. Only going through an experience like this equips, empowers and causes the grace of God to take hold of you. Jesus was betrayed; He showed how to respond to betrayal, rather than to react to it.

I know many reading these words will have been betrayed and some may still be stuck in the hurt of it. Some may still be feeling the wounds and be dealing with the aftermath of such horrendous experiences. My prayer for you is this:

Father, heal Your children. Take them with understanding beyond where they are. I pray they will learn not to 'nurse' the hurt but to 'disperse' it. I command broken hearts to be healed and wounds to be closed. Be comforted and restored in the mighty name of Jesus!

Chapter Nineteen
Celebration

People used to joke that Ashford was 'Trashford'. We've helped to change that.

When we arrived, we arrived to a miracle. The building the church was in was an old car showroom. All sorted and paid for. The congregation had been faithful in their giving over the years. It was a declaration of God's faithfulness – a building in the centre of the town. This building hadn't always been home to the church. They started on one of the notorious estates in Ashford; the first church to build there.

Many churches had failed to take off over the years; ACF was one of the first of the 'new' churches to succeed. And the founders, Syd and Liz, sacrificed much in the establishing of the church against the odds in terms of the spiritual atmosphere of the town at the time. Our church and others have started to change that spiritual atmosphere. It's true to say that today most residents no longer see the place as 'Trashford', but speak well of the town.

As we began to recover from our early mistakes, God began to bless us. We moved to two services on a Sunday. New people were arriving. So much so, we really needed a bigger building. We had our problems, of course, but even so, we look back with gratefulness for all God has done.

'That's your new building'

The showroom was too small, and it was falling apart. Over the years, we had done it up, but it just wasn't going to be a place where we could continue to grow. By 2014, fifteen years after our arrival in the town, we were desperate. I was regularly praying about it and researching every building that might be suitable.

But the fact was, there were no suitable buildings in the centre of the town, and we were not comfortable about moving out from the centre.

One day, in the small office I used at the end of our showroom building, I looked up. There, down the street and across the road, was the grand old Methodist church building. I heard God speak to me: 'David, that's your new building.'

I had prayed about that building many times over the years. But I had dismissed it. There were too many obstacles. Too much money. Too many objections from the Methodists to it being sold. It was a pipe dream.

But surely, I had just heard God's voice? I began to doubt what I had heard. No. God had said!

We began to pray as a church. The building, built in the 1870s, had been on and off the market over the years. At one point, the Methodists had been asking £1.2 million for it. Now it was back on the market at £750,000. It may as well have been the higher price, though, as far as I was concerned, as we just didn't have the money.

We continued to pray.

We were radically obedient.

Along with our trustees, we put our own houses on the line to provide collateral for a loan.

By now we had managed to save £150,000. Nowhere near enough, but from a not too wealthy congregation, it reflected sacrificial giving. A number of friends of our ministry kindly gave, which raised a further £50,000. The figure was slowly rising.

The bank was ready to offer us a mortgage. And then they changed their minds. Then the mortgage was back on again. Then it was off again. So frustrating! In the end, the Christian bank, Kingdom Bank, came to the rescue. The sale of the old showroom building helped us along the way too.

The Methodists were agreeable to selling to us, but were clear they would sell to the highest bidder. We prayed again. We were the only bidders! I felt God direct me to offer £500,000 – quite a lot below the asking price. It was accepted. In fact, due to the amount of work needed on the building, the final price came down by a further £50,000.

Celebration

What a celebration, the day we moved in! Our founders, Syd and Liz, came back for the weekend. It was such a mighty time of worship. God was with us. He had done a miracle. Against the odds, against all logic, we were in an enormous building with a warren of offices behind it. And for a miracle price.

At the end of the meeting, Syd and Liz came over to chat to us.

'David, you do realise, this is the very same building we were thrown out of all those years ago?'

'What do you mean?'

'We had to leave the Methodist movement. That's when we had

to set up our own church. It was this building we had to leave. Hasn't God got a wonderful sense of humour?'

Yes, He has.

The shop

One of the benefits in buying the new building was the shop that came with it. It was just a few doors down on the main street, but it was in a bit of a state. Again, God answered. We were able to get shop fittings at a ridiculously low price. Within a short time, we were ready to open a coffee shop.

It was during this time that a young woman called Stephanie approached me.

'Pastor, can we have a chat?'

'Of course.'

'You won't know this, but as a young girl, I had a dream. I dreamt I was running a coffee shop. And one that reached out to the community with the love of Christ.'

Today the dream has come true. The coffee shop is up and running and is a place of peace for many who call.

Changing the atmosphere

Prayer works. As a church, we have regularly prayed for our town and we have seen the atmosphere change. Prayers have been answered. There's a different feel in Ashford today because of the prayer of ACF and like-minded churches.

A pensioner was shot in the Asda supermarket as he tried to tackle some armed robbers. The bullet ricocheted off his key ring. I felt God point me to the article in the paper and say that he was saved because we were praying for our town.

On one occasion in 2006, a getaway van with more than £1 million in it was found by police in a car park in Ashford. As churches, we truly believe that God is protecting our town and crime will not succeed. There are numerous other examples of thieves and murderers getting caught as and when they come to Ashford.

We are proactive in our prayers. We have had the privilege of praying for our local MP and his wife on many occasions. The prophetess Sharon Stone once spoke to them prophetically and the MP's wife was left asking how Sharon knew so much about her! These occasions helped us to get to know our MP and I was able to send him a message before the election to tell him to prepare for power, and that I felt he would be appointed minister in charge of immigration. His party won and he joined the government front benches – in charge of immigration.

When I wrote, I was also aware of certain accusations against him, and sent him a scripture from Isaiah 54: 'No weapon that is formed against you will succeed; And every tongue that rises against you in judgment you will condemn.'[23]

The second line can be translated as 'every tongue that rises against you in a court of law.' At the time, our MP had potential legal charges against him. But he was completely vindicated and the charges dropped.

At another event, we were able to lead our mayor and mayoress to the Lord. We have a 'destiny tent' available at town events,

23. Verse 17, AMP.

where people will queue to receive a prophecy. As they come out of the tent, many in tears due to the accuracy of the prophetic words, we have people on hand to share about Christ, and to lead them to Him.

God gives us a bigger picture of what is happening in our country too, on occasion. Soon after the bombings in London on 7 July 2005, I felt God prompt me that there would be another attack. I called the church to pray and about fifty of us gathered. The second attack, just fourteen days later, ended in failure as the bombs didn't go off. I'm not saying for one moment that this was just down to our prayers, but I am certain that when we join our prayers with those of other believers, God answers, often in dramatic ways.

All generations

It's not just the nations that have joined ACF, but the generations too. Along with Jay, one of our worship leaders in the church, I had the privilege of helping disciple a teenage girl, seeing her turn from thoughts of suicide and self-harming to a wonderful faith in Christ, reflected in her being one of our youngest members of the Kenyan missions team.

Working with this young lady was a bit of an eye-opener for me. How lost this young generation is! Caught up in endless cyber-world online addictions, hurting, self-harming, watching films and videos from a young age depicting sexual acts.

With Jay's help, we began to show this young lady a different life. She learned to understand a real Father's heart, and a God who loves her unconditionally. She learned to pray and to see the sick healed. She learned to listen to the Spirit's voice and to prophesy. Today, she is one of our musicians, having taught herself both the guitar and keyboards.

She is a reflection of many, as God works to bring a whole new generation into His purposes. Changed. Saved. Baptised. And to still be here to see it is a thrill.

Matt is another youngster we have worked with. I saw an evangelist's ministry in Matt and have personally discipled him. It's important as leaders that we find time for the 'ones and twos'; sometimes they are people that maybe others have rejected. But I know from my own life that God is good at rescuing the seemingly unrescuable. Matt has come through gambling and alcohol additions. He walked away from his faith for a while. But when he came back, he was welcomed by the ACF family as if he had never been away. The welcome he received has helped revolutionise his Christian life. Today he is free of his addictions and regularly works as an evangelist, seeing many find faith in Christ.

Another young lady I have been able to help is Esther. Much can be done with the right use of computers! Esther is in Zambia, and Joyce and I have been able to correspond with her, sending books to help; discipling her online. The result to date is more than 100 teenagers saved through Esther's ministry. And she's still only eighteen!

We try to go the extra mile in seeing people find a faith in Christ, well aware that if they will come into the presence of the Holy Spirit in a church meeting, they are likely to find salvation. Jenny is a case in point. Through a friend, I was called out to a police station to be with her, after she reported a death threat on her life. She was distressed and shaken. I took one of our leaders with me, and together we were able to pray with Jenny, lead her to a faith in Christ and support her in what she was going through.

It turned out that although Jenny looked capable and in charge of her life, that simply wasn't the case. She didn't have the money to travel to our church meetings, so some of our women leaders helped her with that, and regularly called round to support her as she dealt with family loss and alcohol addiction.

In Luke chapter 15 of the Bible, Jesus talks about leaving the ninety-nine sheep and going after the one. The time and energy was well-rewarded. Today Jenny is on fire for the Lord; a great return on the persistence of our leaders.

It's for you as well

As I reflect on my life, I'm grateful that Father God has saved tens of thousands through our ministry; thousands have been healed; thousands baptised in the Holy Spirit. There have been hundreds of outstanding miracles; churches have been planted; pastors and leaders have been empowered and equipped and have seen their churches grow. Towns and cities have been regenerated by God's decree. The most significant effect of God's grace is that the black sheep of the Lamb family became a witness, a leader and a commander. If I had only lived to see God's love and mercy save and redeem my family, especially my precious Mum and Dad, it would have been enough. But with Father God there's always so much more! God chose me; a foolish, wild, sinful man, and made me a champion. I'm still blown away by His outrageous daily mercies to me. What an awesome Father He is.

I want to remind you as the reader, that He is the same God in you as in me. The apostle Peter reminds us that we are *all* part of God's nation, that we are all God's priests and kings.[24] I want to encourage you to recognise what God has made you to be.

Jesus gives us His authority as believers.[25] We can go in that authority and see the situations that we each face completely change as we pray into that situation.

One of our church members began to tell her boss that she was praying for him and for the success of the business. The boss began to notice that each time the lady prayed, the business prospered – so he began to ask her to pray ahead of her offering the prayer!

Another church member was faced with potential redundancy and the closure of her particular branch. As this was work to do with the local community, it meant even more to her that the branch remained open. She started going into work early and quietly praying in the bosses' offices before the rest of the staff arrived. She prayed that there would be no cuts and that the branch would be able to continue with its work in the community. Other parts of the organisation were closed, but the branch was unaffected and there were no cuts or redundancies.

We have a mandate from God to pray and intercede. And when we do, He hears and answers.

---

24. See 1 Peter 2:9-10.
25. See Matthew 28:18-19.

The writer to the Hebrews says that 'every high priest ... is appointed to act on behalf of men in relation to God'.[26] That's you and me. We have that mandate. We have the authority. We can act on behalf of our friends and family. We can intercede for them – and see God answer.

Someone once said that we should pray over our family in the Holy Spirit; we should bind and cast out every demon, and we should ask Father God to send someone to witness to them to whom they will listen. That's good advice. I can't always speak directly to my family about my faith – I'm too close, and often they will be looking at me and thinking of what I used to be like. It gets in the way of the witness. But I can pray. I can bind and cast out. And I can seek God for the right person to speak into their lives.

Let's extend that thinking to our communities and our towns and cities. In Isaiah, God says that our city walls are 'continually before' Him.[27] He has such a heart for our streets, towns and cities. As we pray for them, we can *represent* them. We have that authority to speak on behalf of what we are part of. We can *represent* our towns and villages. We can *represent* our friends and family. And He hears.

Knowing He hears, we can then step out in faith and pray for the opportunity to speak. To speak to those in positions of influence in our villages, towns and cities. To speak to those we are praying for and ask that God blesses our words with His salvation.

---

26. Hebrews 5:1.
27. Isaiah 49:16.

Glory cloud

> And Moses was not able to enter the tent of meeting because the cloud settled on it, and the glory of the Lord filled the tabernacle. (Exodus 40:35)

> And the priests could not enter the house of the Lord, because the glory of the Lord filled the Lord's house. (2 Chronicles 7:2)

There are numbers of references to God's glory cloud coming on His people. In recent times, there have been many who have again seen the cloud in meetings and conferences.

As I stood at the front of the ACF congregation one Sunday, I was aware of a closeness to the heavenly realms. It was clear we were all noticing it. A reverence settled on the congregation and the musicians were struggling to continue to play.

At the back of the room, I saw a cloud, moving forward, covering the people. We continued to worship, unaware of the time.

Two hours later, I felt the presence begin to lift off us and I quietly brought the meeting to an end.

A number of people came up to me afterwards.

'Pastor, why did you stop after such a short time? Why did we stop worshipping after just a few minutes?'

I pointed to the clock on the wall. It had been over two hours. It felt like five minutes.

That morning changed us as a church. We have never been the same again. In most of our worship times, right up to the present, there is preciousness in the worship. Those that were there that day still speak of it as a turning point in their own walk of faith.

When God comes in power, anything is possible. Time becomes irrelevant. Expectations, or a lack of them, are put aside. He is with us. Here to bless. Here to save. Here to change our nation. Here to change the world we live in.

I'm a witness to that. God took a wild man, changed him and took him on wild adventures of faith. He did it. And I'm grateful He did.

This isn't the end of our story. Joyce and I have much ahead of us still. But as I write these final words, I want you to know, He hasn't finished with you either. God is on the move by His Holy Spirit, and you are part of His purposes. He has a plan for you that He doesn't have for me. He thought of you before the beginning of time. He is ready to bless you; fill you with His Spirit. And He is ready to use you, whether you consider yourself an evangelist or not, to change your street, your neighbours, your workmates.

This is our story. What will yours be?

About the Authors

David and Joyce Lamb serve as pastors of Ashford Christian Fellowship. They are regular speakers at Christian events and still travel the world declaring the gospel. You can find the church site at www.acfchurch.org.uk.

Ralph Turner is married to Roh. They have four adult children and two grandchildren. Ralph is team pastor for Mission24 and chair of the Leprosy Mission England & Wales. You can find Ralph's blog at www.mountain50.blogspot.com.